ENWINGYING SCOT

DIONE PATTULLO & DEREK CO

JOHNSTON & BACON

A Johnston & Bacon book published by
Cassell Ltd.
35 Red Lion Square, London WC1R 4SG
and at Sydney, Auckland, Toronto, Johannesburg,
an affiliate of
Macmillan Publishing Co., Inc.,
New York

© Derek Cooper and Dione Pattullo, 1980

First published 1980

ISBN 0 7179 4256 2

Set, printed and bound in Great Britain by
Fakenham Press Limited, Fakenham, Norfolk

Contents

The Water of Life

Two hundred years ago making whisky in Scotland was a cottage industry that flourished in every island and almost every glen. That it was illegal made the operation infinitely more attractive. The remote possibility that an exciseman might come riding over the hill and confiscate your still lent an element of sport to the proceedings.

While the man about the house was out catching fish for the pot, the wife could well be baking a few barley bannocks or more likely converting the barley into something more spirituous. Like bingo, it was a game everyone could play. Travelling round the Highlands in the 1770's, the zoologist and traveller Thomas Pennant, noted the 'ruinous distillation' that prevailed in Islay and the lack of barley in Kintyre. 'Notwithstanding the quantity raised, there is often a sort of dearth; the inhabitants being mad enough to convert their bread into poison, distilling annually six thousand bolls of grain into whisky.'

The Duke of Argyll, the principal proprietor, was at some pains to discourage this pernicious practice but the profit was so great that few were able to resist the joys of elevating an uninteresting mash of malt into *Uisge Beatha*, the Water of Life.

At Campbeltown in Kintyre a still could be bought complete with worm, arm and head for £5 and would easily pay for itself within three months. In the remote islands of the Hebrides where revenue men ran risk of grievous bodily harm if they showed themselves, distilling became big business. The small island of Tiree exported up to three thousand gallons a year and Islay teemed with smugglers' bothies.

Even if you didn't make it yourself illicit whisky was easy to come by and at about 5d a bottle, unburdened by excise duty, barley bree became as accepted a part of life as herrings and oatmeal brose. At weddings and funerals whisky flowed like fiery water and anyone who called at a house had a dram instantly poured down him. By the beginning of the nineteenth century probably half the whisky drunk in Scotland was made by smugglers. Like the illegal manufacture of moonshine in Ireland 'few industries gave so much employment, none gave more pleasure.'

Eventually illicit distillation became so rife that, in 1823, the government was forced to relax its repressive legislation and the more substantial smugglers were encouraged, with the duty on whisky halved, to take out licences. Legal distilleries rose on the site of illicit bothies and what had been a clandestine and unlawful occupation grew respectable and highly profitable. Distillers were raised to the peerage and today whisky has become Scotland's number one export.

But it remains an industry with its roots buried deeply in the remote countryside where, tucked away from the predatory eye of the revenue men, whisky used to be made in stealthy seclusion. All you needed really was a cold running burn and peats to fire the still. So even today you will find many distilleries perched on the banks of rivers or near the source of clear fresh springs. Water-power is no longer used to drive the machinery but the water itself, as we shall see, is still all-important. Other distilleries lie on the coastline, often sited at the mouth of a burn, and you can be sure that in the old days many of them had a lookout stationed on a headland, an eye skinned for the sails of a patrolling revenue cutter. Once sighted the still would be dismantled and the vital copper worm which condensed the spirit would be smuggled away into the hills until the coast was once again clear.

Back to the grass roots

I thought it might be a good idea to find out if the making of whisky had changed very much since the eighteenth century and, more important, tell you how it is made. But where to go? To the Hebrides which in the days of the clans was reputed to make the best whisky of all, or to the Spey Valley where that most famous of all malts, Glenlivet, had its origin? Or perhaps north to Orkney, or to the east coast, or to the Lowlands? There are a hundred and fifteen malt distilleries to choose from, and most of them have been distilling for well over a century.

I decided to go to Islay to see how the 'ruinous distillation' was getting on in the age of the microchip. If the Spey Valley is the Bordeaux of whisky then Islay is its Burgundy, renowned not only for the antiquity of its distilleries—Lagavulin was established in 1742—but for their diversity and distinctive flavour. None is more distinctive than Laphroaig, as famous in Scotland as Lafite or Latour are in France.

I choose Laphroaig not only because it happens to be one of my five favourite malts, but because it is one of the handful of distilleries left in Scotland which still malts some of its barley in the traditional manner using time-honoured techniques.

Islay is only twenty-five minutes by Loganair from that great centre of whisky blending and bottling, Glasgow. We fly in the little Trislander down the Clyde. It's a bitterly cold February morning, ideal weather for distilling, the Renfrew moors are snow-covered and the late-rising sun bathes them in a cochineal pink light. In minutes we're over Bute with the Isle of Arran on the port wing and the long thin Kintyre peninsula dusted with sparkling snow like icing sugar. Then Gigha, only six miles long with its famous gardens of Achamore ablaze in the spring and summer with rhododendrons, azaleas and hydrangeas. Across the open glass-flat sea and there lies Islay, southernmost of the Inner Hebrides.

As we leave the airport a van arrives with boxes of lobsters for the five-star restaurants of Paris. Islay is noted for its cheese too but it is the eight distilleries—

Ardbeg, Bowmore, Bruichladdich, Bunnahabhain, Caol Ila, Lagavulin, Port Ellen and Laphroaig—that have made it internationally famous.

We drive from the airport past the peat banks that give the Islay malts part of their characteristic flavour and then in ten minutes or so we turn right through a wooded coppice and there lying at the water's edge are the buildings of Laphroaig, surrounded by trim lawns and a seashore garden.

The manager, Denis Nicol, sits in an office from which on a clear day he can see Ireland. It is crystal clear today, the sun burning down from the blue winter sky.

'That's actually Rathlin you can see, with the coast of Ireland beyond.'

Islay has always had close connections with Ireland, and it is from Ireland that the secret of the art of distillation is said to have originally come. The Irish called it *usquebaugh* and the word 'whisky' itself, or 'whiskey' as the Irish spell it, is a corruption of the Gaelic word for water: *uisge*.

'We still have a connection with Ireland. There's a boat at the pier in Port Ellen just now unloading a cargo of malt for us.'

Legally you can make Scotch whisky out of barley grown anywhere in the world, but if you took barley grown in Scotland to Japan or Australia you couldn't produce Scotch malt whisky there. The distillation must be done in Scotland.

Technical treatises have been written on the mysteries of distilling, but I've come to Laphroaig to have it explained as simply as possible by a man who makes 16,000 gallons of whisky a week. But first a look at the works. The traditional distillery in Scotland is built of stone and its whitewashed walls are four-square and solid. Laphroaig, its Gaelic name means the Hollow of Proig, still has many of its old buildings—its barley-barn and maltings and its tall kiln three stories high with concave-slated roof rising to the familiar pagoda-shaped cowls through which the peat smoke escapes like acrid incense. Then there's the Mash House, the Tun Room, the Still House and the warehouses where the equivalent of £5 million worth of whisky lies silently maturing. If the duty is included it works out at around £180 million worth. As you walk round the distillery your nostrils receive a succession of scents. There's always ozone in the air, particularly when a wind is blowing off the sea; there's the strong pungent smell of burning peat, the damp mushroomy mustiness of the germinating barley, the sweet, almost sickly, aroma of fermenting malt, the heady fumes of distillation.

Whisky is made by mashing malted barley with hot water, adding yeast and then distilling it two or sometimes three times in an onion-shaped copper still, and there are many who believe that it is the soft and peaty waters that make the best mashes.

On Islay the distilleries guard their water sources with almost obsessional care. Ardbeg, built in 1815, takes its water from Loch Arinambeast and Loch Uigidale; the site on the verge of the sea had long been a haunt of smugglers who used those very same sources of water. Bowmore, which was founded in 1779, draws on the River Laggan. Caol Ila, built in 1846, was established on the Sound of Islay, facing Jura, so that it could take advantage of the crystal clear waters of Loch Torrabus. Bunnahabhain, built in 1881, uses the soft peaty water of a stream fed by Loch Staoinsha, and Laphroaig has equally valuable sources.

'Our water comes from the Kilbride river which has as its main source Loch na Beinn Brice.' The river flows over peatbogs to the distillery. 'If you want to be technical', says Denis, a chemist by training, 'it has a Ph of 6.8; that's slightly acidic. There's quite a lot of humus in it and limonite, a bog-iron ore.'

Half a mile down the road is the almost equally well-known distillery of Lagavulin, which provides one of the ingredients of the White Horse blend made popular by Sir Peter Mackie. Restless Peter, as he was known, took over Lagavulin in 1888, and with it the agency for Laphroaig. According to Denis Nicol, the owner of Laphroaig Alexander Johnston, fell out with Mackie who chopped off his water supply. 'So Johnston sued White Horse for the restoration of his rights and he won the case. Well Mackie was a bit of a character and he said "Right, if you won't sell us Laphroaig we'll build a Laphroaig-type distillery inside Lagavulin and make our own!"'

Mackie set his men to work and, half a mile away, they built two stills which were exact replicas of the ones in Laphroaig. He even went to the lengths of poaching the brewer from Laphroaig, but when the spirit came off the stills it was not Laphroaig. The water was the same, the stills were identical but somehow Laphroaig refused to be duplicated.

There are many similar stories in Scotland. The family of Grant who built the Glenfiddich distillery in 1886 established in 1890 a second distillery close by, to which they gave the name Balvenie. Although the two distilleries use the same malt and water from the Robbie Dubh spring their whiskies are quite different.

In the Highland capital of Inverness there are two distilleries using water from the River Ness, Glen Albyn and Glen Mhor. They are both owned by the same company but once again they produce an entirely different malt. And then there is Glen Grant, the oldest distillery in the Spey Valley, built in 1840 at Rothes. In 1897 the family built a new distillery on the other side of the road which they called Glen Grant No. 2. But although it used water from the same burn as Glen Grant it refused to be number two to anybody and when its first whisky matured it turned out to be something quite unique.

'When Ian Hunter ran the distillery, and he took it over when his mother died in 1928, he was at great pains not to tarmac the road where a pipe carrying water ran under it. He was afraid that the tar might leech into the ground and have some adverse effect on the water which might in turn affect the spirit.'

The next variable is the barley. You can't use just any old barley to make whisky, it has to have certain qualities. In the old days all the grain used in whisky-making was grown in Scotland. The finest Highland barley came from the rich black soil of what is known as the Laigh of Moray on the east coast. Today whisky makers also import their barley from Canada, Ireland, East Anglia and even Australia.

Barley, particularly when grown in Scotland, varies from season to season depending on the conditions at the time of harvesting. To make whisky you first have to convert your barley into something called malt and to do that is not all that easy.

First of all you steep the barley in water. 'It's not just pouring water on and hoping for the best. You've got to consider all sorts of things. You may have to steep the barley for twelve hours and then let it air-rest for twelve hours and then resteep it for another twelve hours.'

When barley is harvested in the field it may contain up to 25% moisture. It is then taken into the maltings and dried down to 12%. Important too is the nitrogen content of the barley; the more nitrogen the less starch and consequently the less sugar, and it is from the sugar that the alcohol is made.

Most distilleries have long since abandoned malting their own barley. It was simple and logical in Victorian times when very often a distillery had its own farm and a plentiful supply of farm labourers. Today almost all the malt used in distilling is processed mechanically in centralised maltings and then despatched by road or rail to the distillery.

But Laphroaig still uses its own floor maltings and 45% of its whisky is distilled from malt actually converted from barley on the spot. The rest comes from Ireland and East Lothian.

'The barley we use comes in "dressed" but it's never

as clean as we want it. We take an 8-ton load of barley and put it through a dressing machine. The broken husks, the straw, the culms, the stones, things like that are all removed. Then it goes into a conical steep and we add about 1500 gallons of water to it.'

The water varies in temperature from 40 °F in winter to 60° in summer. 'Obviously temperature affects the uptake. The warmer the water the more rapid the absorption. In very cold weather you steep it for a bit longer.'

At Laphroaig they have a rough rule of thumb for deciding how long the barley should be allowed to steep. 'You take a figure of 110 and subtract the temperature of the water. If it's 60° you'd steep for fifty hours; if it's 40° you'd steep for seventy hours. But what you have to do is hit the magical figure of 44% moisture.'

The steep is then drained for an hour and the moist barley is ready for laying on the malting floor. 'Some of the floors are tiled, some are slated, but they're never made of wood because over the years the wet barley would just rot them. Ours are made of concrete.'

At Laphroaig the malting floors are 100 feet long and 50 feet wide, and over these the barley is spread with brushes to a depth of 4 or 5 inches.

Malting

Now comes the most crucial stage. As the moist barley lies on the floor it begins to absorb oxygen from the air, release carbon dioxide and generate heat. The deeper the malt is piled the more heat it engenders.

'If it's very cold,' says Denis Nicol, 'as it is just now, you may heap the malt higher; that's called "couching" and it starts chitting more rapidly. On the other hand in hot weather, if the temperature goes up to the seventies and eighties, you may have to keep turning the barley to prevent it from growing too rapidly. Malting is really a winter sport.'

What happens on the floor is a biological conversion. The barley begins to germinate and, as it grows and sprouts, the barley starch is converted into malt starch, a modification undertaken by enzymes. After a week or so this process will be completed and the malt ready. 'You can tell whether it's ready or not by taking a grain and crushing it between your finger and thumb. If it's ready it should have a powdery feel and you should be able to chalk your name with it on the wall.'

During the week that the barley is germinating the maltmen will turn it daily, sometimes twice a day, to expose it to the cooling air and prevent the rootlets from matting together.

Although, as I've said, there are very few distilleries actually converting their barley into malt by spreading it on floors, an identical and less labour-intensive process is achieved in Saladin boxes or drum maltings where the barley is aerated and exposed to the optimum temperature and humidity, either in automatically controlled troughs or in huge perforated drums. Whichever method is adopted it is essential to halt the process of germination at the right moment; if growth were allowed to continue, roots and leaves would develop and enzymes would liquidise the starch, consuming the maltose produced in their cycle of self-nourishment. So when the acrospire (first leaf) has grown to about three-quarters the length of the barleycorn the green malt is transferred to a drying kiln.

The pagoda-shaped kilns with their pungent smell of burning peat were for many years the most characteristic feature of a distillery, and even now when they lie unused they form a strong visual link with the past. At Laphroaig they are still very much in use and the distillery has 150 acres of peat moss at Glen Egedale to feed the kilns, enough to last for a hundred years. The peats are cut between February and July and when the pitch black slabs are first laid out to dry they are almost as soft as butter, being 90% water. By the time the wind has dried them out the moisture has been reduced

to about 10% and they are then brought to the distillery by tractor and stored in the peat shed.

The floor of the kiln is made of perforated wedge
wire and the malt is spread over this mesh to a depth of
fifteen inches. Then a peat fire is lit on the hearth
below and the peat-reek rises and percolates through
the green malt, both flavouring it and drying it.

'What you are getting absorbed into the malt are the
steam-volatile phenols, the pyrolyed lignium compounds, the aromatic carbon molecules, the phenols
cresols, xylenols, things like that. As the malt dries it
becomes less receptive to the phenols, and after about
twenty-four hours the smoke begins to go straight
through the malt. At that stage we give it a final drying
off with hot air and after another twenty-four hours the
moisture content has dropped to four or five per cent.'

There is no whisky in Scotland more heavily peated
than Laphroaig, and to produce this intense aroma in
the malt you need the old-fashioned kiln in which the
smoke rises naturally and slowly and permeates every
individual barley-corn. In the new mechanical maltings
the peat smoke is blown through the green malt by
fans and high concentrations of phenols cannot be so
easily achieved.

Running a floor malting is not only hard work—the
spreading and turning are all done by hand using old-
fashioned malt barrows like Roman chariots, and heavy
wooden spades called 'shiels'—it also calls for constant
supervision. The length of time the barley takes to
germinate depends on a variety of external factors for
which it is not always easy to compensate. In bitterly
cold weather the maltsters may have difficulty in
persuading the barley to germinate; in a heat wave the
process can be equally difficult to control.

So none of the distilleries built in recent years have
floor maltings and throughout Scotland the old floor
maltings have either been converted to other uses or
demolished.

Even distilleries which persevere with their floor

maltings find that increased output means they must buy a certain amount of malt from outside sources. Laphroaig is no exception. 'We take malt both from Eire and the mainland. The barley malted in Ireland is very heavily peated but the malt we get from our suppliers Hugh Baird in Pencaitland is not peated at all. We use a mix: 45% of our own malt, $27\frac{1}{2}$% Irish malt, and $27\frac{1}{2}$% mainland.'

When the malt has been dried it looks almost the same as it did when it arrived in the distillery in the form of barley. But it is crisp and friable and has a smoky sweet taste. Ideally the malt should now be put aside to rest for up to six weeks in storage bins: 'Nobody knows why but you get far better extracts from malt that has been allowed to lie in this way.'

So whisky requires water in abundance and a plentiful supply of malt. What next?

The next stage could be done in an old bucket but in distilleries mashing the malt is carried out in huge tanks, rather like giant Dundee cake tins, called mash tuns. Before the malt is mashed it is screened and cleaned. The broken malt, the dried rootlets, the husk are sieved out, and any metal objects that may have found their way into the malt are removed magnetically —a spark during the milling process when the air is thick with malt dust could cause a dangerous explosion.

Then the crushed malt is ground in a four-roll Porteous mill, forty kilos at a time. Ideally it should be a coarse grind: 20% husk, 70% grits or meal and no more than 10% flour. Too finely-ground malt interferes with the drainage rate of the mash. Once the malt is ground, it becomes hygroscopic, and when it picks up moisture it can go 'slack,' as they say in distilleries, so grinding occurs immediately before the mashing.

The mash

At Laphroaig they use 6.88 metric tons of grist, as the malt is now called, for every mash. The grist is carried to a hopper above the mash tun where it is released and mixed mechanically with 5500 gallons of water which has been pre-heated to 150 °F. The function of mashing is to leach all the sugar from the grist so that it will convert readily into alcohol. The starch-reducing enzymes peck away in the warmth of the porridgy mash for about an hour and then the liquor is drained off through the perforated bottom into a storage tank called an 'underback' or 'washback.'

More hot water is added to the residue in the mash tun to leach out yet more sugar, and the cycle of mashing reuses these waters economically until the maximum amount of sugar has been extracted. The chilled liquor collected in the washback from the first and second waters makes one 'charge.' At Laphroaig they have nine washbacks, six of 5000-gallon capacity and three holding 9000 gallons. The mashing cycle begins every twelve hours and carries on for seven days a week.

Left behind after the mashing is a wet mess known as 'draff.' It contains a minimum of sugars, but when it is dried it produces what is known as 'distillers light grains,' popular with farmers as a base for cattle feed.

By now we have achieved a rather unpleasant sweet, amber-coloured liquid, called 'wort,' which has been cooled to about 70 °F before the next vital stage.

Adding the yeast

About $2\frac{1}{2}$ hundredweight of yeast is added to the washback when filling begins, and immediately fermentation starts. This process, in which the wort can boil and foam with excitement, releases large amounts of carbon dioxide and begins to produce alcohol. After about two days, during which time the wort is carefully monitored by the brewer, the process halts itself —the alcohol produced by the yeast exists in sufficient quantities to inhibit further metamorphosis: the

Malted barley germinating on a malting floor. Laphroaig is one of the few distilleries which still carries out its own maltings.

Copper stills at Laphroaig

creamy brew gradually stops working and bubbling. So far the process is not all that dissimilar to the making of beer.

The wort that contained $12\frac{1}{2}\%$ sugar has been converted into a wash which is $11\frac{1}{2}°$ proof spirit and it is at this stage that, if you were making whisky for yourself, the exciseman would begin to take a keen interest. What I have not yet mentioned is that distilling whisky isn't quite as unfettered as making parsnip wine.

If you want to start distilling whisky you will first of all have to get the plan of your distillery approved by the Commissioners of the Board of Customs and Excise. They will also wish to inspect all your vessels and utensils, your pipes and fittings. They will expect you to provide a room with washing facilities for their exciseman and, if you have decided to build your distillery in a remote part of the landscape, they have the power to force you to build a house for him and his family. And you will also have to pay an annual licence fee of £15.75. H.M. Customs and Excise take a very protective interest in the whisky industry. In 1978 it yielded £512 million in duty, so not a dram must go unaccounted for; the only whisky which escapes taxation is the 2% or so which evaporates each year during maturation and the vast quantities which go for export.

Everywhere in a distillery you will see the double locks that mark the exciseman's control: one belonging to the Excise, one to the distiller. The warehouses cannot be opened without the exciseman's key turning in the second lock, and when the whisky is put into cask he is there to measure every last drop. Both the distiller and the resident exciseman know how much whisky should be produced from a given amount of malt. At Laphroaig one mash should ideally furnish 1000 gallons of proof whisky—if only 950 gallons come off the still the manager is going to be disappointed and the exciseman suspicious.

The distillation

The wash contains the raw material which will eventually be distilled into whisky; the next step is to pump it from the Tun Room to the Still House for the first stages of distillation. At Laphroaig they have three copper wash stills, each capable of taking 2400 gallons. The wash will be boiled in much the same way as water is boiled in a kettle; the vapours that rise will then be cooled and condensed into what are known as 'low wines.'

The indirectly oil-fired stills contain stainless steel coils through which the superheated steam circulates, and although stills vary in size from 750 gallons to 3000 gallons, depending on the distillery, their function is the same. Because alcohol has a lower boiling point than water it is the first vapour to ascend from the boiling wash; it rises first into the neck of the still, then it is channelled through a pipe called the lyne arm into the condenser.

In the early days of distilling the apparatus which condensed the vapours was a coiled tube of copper, of gradually decreasing width, cooled by running water. Known as the 'worm,' this was the most essential tool of the smuggler. Today the worm is usually a highly efficient heat exchanger. The lyne arm, the pipe which connects the head of the still to the condenser, also plays a vital part in the speed and quality of the condensation.

If the arm is rising upwards into the condenser then the 'reflux' will be greater—more of the vapours will fall back into the neck of the still; but if the arm is sloping downwards into the condenser, noticeably more compounds will be carried forward into the condensing distillate.

I have been told that there are distilleries which have their lyne arms on a pulley so that they can vary the product according to the individual demands of their customers, but that may be malicious gossip. Whatever the angle of the lyne arm in the wash still, the spirit which is condensed is very oily and crude with plenty of fusel-oil floating on its surface. A third of the volume of the wash is collected in this way and the unfermentable residue either goes to waste or is processed into pot ale syrup. At Laphroaig the pot ale or burnt ale is discharged into the sea, but many inland distilleries process their residue into high-protein animal foodstuffs, while others take it by tanker to the nearest sewage farm.

At this stage the low wines, impure and containing only about 30% alcohol, are an extremely unpalatable and unpotable liquid. From the wash still they are taken by pipe through a spirit safe to the low wines and feints receiver. The spirit safe is a large brass glass-walled box which is kept permanently locked by the exciseman. In many ways it is like the Tantalus which used to sit on Victorian sideboards: the servants could see the spirit in the decanters but only the butler had the key. In the distillery the exciseman has the key but the stillman by an ingenious system of external taps can channel the spirit wherever he wants it. He can add water to it to test it for purity and, using jars containing hydrometers, he can measure the specific gravity of the spirit.

The spirit still

To purify the low wines still further, they are then piped to a spirit still. Spirit stills are usually smaller than wash stills because they have a smaller quantity of liquid to deal with. At Laphroaig there are three 800-gallon spirit stills and one of 1600 gallons. Here is enacted the final distillation that produces whisky. Once the vapours begin to rise in the spirit still and condense down the pipe into the spirit safe the stillman is constantly monitoring the distillation.

First of all come what are quite appropriately called the 'foreshots,' and they are usually 130° proof. The stillman, using his taps, channels these into the blue-painted pipe that will carry them back to the low wines and feints receiver. Every now and again he will mix the foreshots with water at 80° proof to record the progress of the distillation. As soon as the foreshots come into contact with water the heavy oils turn the water a cloudy milky colour. The stillman will keep testing for perhaps an hour until the foreshots, when mixed with water, run crystal clear; he knows then that pure spirit is coming off the still and, quickly turning his taps, he directs the flow into the intermediate spirits receiver.

The foreshots begin to clear at about 122° proof and the stillman will then allow the spirit to run for 2 to $2\frac{1}{2}$ hours until it begins to weaken to 108° proof when he makes the final cut, diverting the rest of the spirit, or 'feints' as the after shots are known, back into the low wines and feints receiver.

Even in the most modern automated distillery the 'fractionation'—the moment when you separate foreshots from spirit and spirit from feints—is still a critical operation. 'When you are running your foreshots,' Denis Nicol tells me, 'you can run the still reasonably quickly, but as soon as you are on spirit you cut down the speed because you want a *slow* production. Hammer the still too hard and you will push more of the oils over. You need a delicate flow in the middle.'

As soon as the feints have ceased to run the stillman is left with a watery residue. The distillation is stopped and the residue or 'spent lees' is discharged into the sewer.

There is much debate about the mystery or art of distilling. Certainly the substances which appear in the whisky—the aldehydes, fusel-oil, furfural—play an important part in its taste and flavour. The shape of the still, even the way it is fired, the speed of 'cooking' the wash, the temperature of the still, the volume of the all-important 'middle cut,' all these are variables which are believed to affect the quality of the whisky.

And indeed the often remarkable differences between the product of one still and another make the almost fanatical concern to reproduce a new still identical in every respect to the old one it replaces understandable. If the shape of the still actually shapes the whisky then a preoccupation with shapes is highly laudable. Many stillmen regard their stills like teapots; just as it is popularly supposed that a new pot doesn't make good tea so a still is thought to improve with age.

When in 1923 it was decided to increase production at Laphroaig and add two new stills, they were exact replicas of two which had been installed in 1882. Stills which are subjected to great heat over prolonged periods of time tend to wear out fairly quickly but very often, rather than replace a treasured still, coppersmiths will be called in to repair it until it becomes as patched as a tinker's kettle or granny's quilt.

A still may well last for fifteen to twenty years but some parts, like the swan neck, which is exposed to corrosion from the ascending vapour, may need replacing long before that. To make a new still, elaborate measurements are made of the existing one so that the exact curves of the old can be reproduced in the new. It may take up to $2\frac{1}{2}$ months to complete a still, and these days the bill may be anything up to £30,000.

The new spirit is colourless, raw, fiery and rough; whisky certainly in nature if not in refinement. At Laphroaig they make eighty or so distillations a week and the spirit is collected in batches of 5000 gallons. 'Although we hope that every distillation is perfect, if for any reason you did get a distillation below average it would not really have much ill effect, because something like twenty-seven separate distillations are blended together before the whisky is filled into cask.'

No spirit can be called whisky until it is three years old, and all whisky has to be matured by law in oak casks. For decades these casks were sold to the trade by sherry shippers who imported their wine from Jerez in wooden butts. Once they had bottled their sherry they were quite happy to pass the barrels on to the whisky distilleries.

In the old days when distillation was apt to be un-scientific and erratic and the spirit could vary wildly from week to week, a sherry cask could overwhelm these differences. An inferior whisky could also be masked by maturing it in a sherry butt. These days that is no longer necessary.

Sherry-impregnated oak imparted both colour and flavour to the whisky, and there is no doubt that the malt whiskies made fifty years ago were frequently sweeter and darker than the whiskies of today; some were matured in madeira casks. Now that sherry is imported in bulk, casks are becoming both rare and expensive. Some distilleries still treat their casks with a wine preparation, but these days the role of wine in maturing whisky is diminishing.

At Laphroaig, as in many other distilleries, the whisky is filled mainly into American oak casks. The U.S. government have a law, originally introduced to give employment to their coopers, which makes it illegal to use a bourbon cask more than once, so many of the surplus casks are shipped across the Atlantic to Scotland.

Choosing the warehouse

It is popularly believed in the industry that the place where a whisky is matured has a marked influence on its final taste. An earth floor is thought to be preferable to a concrete floor, a damp and humid warehouse better than a dry one. These days, when much of Scotland's whisky lies maturing in vast Lowland ware-houses with the barrels stacked twelve high, perhaps such subtleties seem academic.

All Islay whiskies take many years to mellow, but what goes on in the barrel here or in Speyside or at Highland Park in Orkney or Talisker in Skye, is some-thing of a mystery. It is certainly a process that cannot be speeded up or reproduced chemically. As the whisky reacts with the air, 'breathing' through the oak staves of the barrel, it achieves a smoothness and roundness which makes it an altogether more benign liquid than the raw whisky which was filled into the barrel straight from the spirit receiver.

One in every five barrels lying in the Laphroaig warehouses belongs to private customers who lay down 'fillings,' as they're known, for use in their own blends. Laphroaig has so distinctive a flavour, almost medicinal in its peatiness, that the amount added to a blend may be very small, sometimes as little as 1%.

The taste of malt

The malt whiskies of Scotland have been traditionally divided into four categories: the eight from Islay; the eleven Lowland malts; the two Campbeltown malts; and the ninety-five Highland malts.

Islay

Each has its own characteristic flavour but in general the Islay malts are considered among the 'heaviest'. In Victorian times that great whisky expert Alfred Barnard, who in his day visited every brewery and distillery in Great Britain and Ireland, declared emphatically 'Islay whisky from its roundness and fatness, is essentially superior to all whiskies of its class for blending . . . it is just as impossible to make good Cognac without Champagne brandy as it is to make a good blend without Islay whisky.'

Campbeltown

The Kintyre peninsula was a centre of illicit distilling and smuggling in the eighteenth century and much of this trade centred on Campbeltown. At the height of its legal boom in the late nineteenth century, Campbeltown had no less than thirty distilleries producing a whisky which was thought by many to be thin, but as

Barnard said, 'a useful whisky at the price.' Today only two distilleries survive, the 156-year-old Springbank which produces a light, enjoyable whisky, and Glen Scotia which began distilling in 1832 and makes a heavy, fairly peaty malt.

Lowland malts

In 1786 Scotland's whisky industry was bisected by parliament into two parts: Highland and Lowland. In England and the Lowlands duty on whisky was collected on the amount of spirit produced; in the Highlands you paid a flat rate based on the capacity of the still. It was an Act intended to check the export of Lowland whisky to England, but it engendered discontent and a national increase in illicit distilling. Today the 'Highland Line' is a mythical boundary that runs roughly from Greenock to Dundee, and the output of the distilleries to the south of it, mainly clustered round Glasgow and Edinburgh, are used almost entirely for blending. Only four of them (Auchentoshan, Bladnoch, Littlemill and Rosebank) are bottled unblended. Barnard was dismissive about Lowland malts. 'The best makes,' he wrote, 'are useful as padding, when they have considerable age and not too much flavour, for they not only help to keep down the price of a blend, but are decidedly preferable to using a large quantity of grain spirit.'

Quicker maturing than most Highland and Island malts, there is perhaps a justification for describing most of the Lowland whiskies as 'silent malts'—they add to the bulk and harbour no unwelcome stridencies.

Highland malts

The heart of Highland distilling is centred round the River Spey as it flows north east from Grantown to the Moray Firth. It's a river noted for salmon, but even more for the famous names in malt which lie along its banks and in the glens of the tributaries which run into Strathspey from the Monadhliath and Cairngorm mountains. The whisky towns of Elgin, Rothes and Dufftown are surrounded by distilleries, old and new.

Here, in this golden rectangle, the really great malts are made: The Glenlivet, Glen Grant, Glenfiddich, Mortlach, Tamnavulin, Linkwood, Longmorn, Macallan, Glenfarclas, Aberlour, Cardow, Knockando, Balmeanach. Although Speyside has the greatest concentration of distilleries in the world, there are well-known names scattered all over the map. Along the eastern coastal area, north of Inverness, lie distilleries like Pulteney, Clynelish, Glenmorangie, Balblair, Teaninich and Royal Brackla. Within striking distance of Aberdeen are Glenury-Royal, Fettercairn, Lochnagar and Glengarioch.

Clustered in the Perth area are Blair Athol, Aberfeldy, Glenturret and Tullibardine. The Highland capital of Inverness has three malt distilleries, Glen Albyn, Glen Mhor and Millburn; and the West Highland capital of Fort William has two, Glenlochy and Ben Nevis.

Although each of the 115 malt distilleries has its mashing tuns, washbacks, wash and spirit stills and ware-houses, in size they range from the minute to the mighty. The smallest distillery in Scotland is Edradour which was built in 1835, near the fashionable Victorian health spa of Pitlochry.

At the other extreme, some sixteen miles south of Inverness is the largest malt distillery in the world, Tomatin, whose eleven stills can produce more than 5 million gallons a year, some of which is exported in bulk to Japan to lend distinction to the whiskies made by Suntory.

The new distilleries

To cope with increasing demand, several highly automated distilleries have been built in the postwar years. They lack the historical associations of the older distilleries, the romance and legend that has grown up over the years, but they are hyper-efficient and frequently make very good malt indeed. None of the new distilleries produce an idiosyncratic malt; that is not the purpose for which they were designed. The bulk of their output is used for innocuous blending, and in blending an ability to harmonise is more valuable than the egregious qualities of the classic malts.

Tullibardine, converted in the late 'forties from a brewery; Glenkeith and Lochside, built in the 'fifties; Macduff, Tomintoul, Ladyburn, Loch Lomond, Tamnavulin and Glenallachie, products of the whisky explosion in the 'sixties; Mannochmore, Braes of Glenlivet, Auchroisk, and Pittyvaich-Glenlivet which came on stream in the 'seventies, are all in the million-gallon-and-more class.

Typical of this new generation of distilleries is Tormore, the first purpose-built malt distillery of this century. The work of the late Sir Albert Richardson, President of the Royal Academy, its sturdy rustic-stone quoined buildings were designed to be operated by the smallest possible labour force. When the first spirit came off the stills in 1959 it had an annual capacity of 300,000 gallons. Today the twenty-four employees at Tormore produce 1,250,000 gallons a year.

Tormore is not exactly what you would call a push-button distillery but it needs only two men per shift, the minimum allowed by industrial legislation, to control the entire process from mashing to final distillation. Old-timers in the whisky trade may shake their heads with dismay at the mention of transistorised consoles and electronic circuits, but has the whisky suffered? Has technology taken art and the heart out of the malt?

Most people would say that the modern distillery has done the reverse. It has brought consistency to the product and a quality-control lacking in the past. In any case comparisons are difficult to make. Over the years popular taste has changed dramatically. The malt whiskies drunk in Victorian and Edwardian times were by all accounts, much heavier, rougher whiskies, very often containing substances which the contemporary brewer is at pains to avoid.

The silent season

In the old days production was still greatly dependent on the seasons, and there came a time in the summer when distilling had to be abandoned altogether. The weather grew too warm for malting, the burns began to run dry, and most distilleries closed for several months in the middle of the year. The 'silent season,' as it was known, was used for maintenance and repairs, and distilling would not begin again until the cool days of autumn.

Distilleries like Laphroaig still have a residual silent season. In August the distillery is closed for four weeks, and again for ten days over Christmas and Hogmanay. It's a point worth remembering if you are planning a tour of distilleries in high summer—you may be able to see over them but you might not see any whisky actually being made.

The single malt

It is only in the last twenty years or so that malt whisky has become widely available. Until then the sale of a malt was usually confined to the area of production. The postwar marketing drive was spearheaded by William Grant & Sons who began to export large amounts of their Glenfiddich overseas, and they now dominate the export market. But the following malt whiskies can all be obtained in bottle at various strengths and ages:

Aberlour, Ardbeg, Aultmore, Balvenie, Balblair, Blair Athol, Bruichladdich, Bowmore, Cardhu, Clynelish,

Dufftown Glenlivet, Dalmore, Deanston Mill, Glen Grant, Glenmorangie, Glenfarclas, Glengarioch, Glengoyne, Glendronach, Glenrothes, Glenleven, Glendullan, Glenury-Royal, Highland Park, Inchgower, Jura, Knockando, Lagavulin, Linkwood, Laphroaig, Lochnagar, Longmorn, Milton Duff, Mortlach, Macallans, Oban, Old Pulteney, Old Fettercairn, Rosebank, Springbank, Strathisla, The Glenlivet, Talisker, Tormore, Tomintoul, Tamdhu, Tamnavulin, Tomatin, Tullibardine.

The importance of age

By law, all whisky must be matured for a minimum of three years, and indeed if expediency were the only interest many distilleries might well be tempted to sell their malt whisky as soon as they legally could. Storage costs are high and the capital invested in the maturing of whisky is prodigious. But it is a fact of life that few malt whiskies are at their best before they have lain at least five years in wood, and many take twice and three times as long to achieve their peak.

Whisky left too long in the barrel can become so woody that it is unpleasant on the palate. So it needs constant surveillance and judicious racking: 'You might start off with ten barrels which would eventually be racked into seven barrels and those seven, after another eight years in wood, could be put into five barrels. And that's expensive.'

There are malts which are at their best after eight years in oak, and eight or ten years nowadays seems to be the marketing norm. Nevertheless it is possible to buy much older whiskies, provided you are prepared to pay a premium price for their rarity, and provided you are aware that old can often mean *too* old!

John and Wallace Milroy, who have in London's Soho the biggest selection of malt whiskies in the world, tell me that they have Glenfarclas, Glenlossie, Glen Grant, Highland Park, Linkwood, Mortlach and

Talisker all at 21 years old, and a few magnums of 25-year-old Macallan's which are going for a modest £45 each.

When you buy a malt whisky you are frequently faced with a choice of ages and 'proofs,' so it might be useful if we defined just what 'proof' is.

Proof

Proof is a method of describing how much alcohol a liquid contains. In this country we have always used the Sikes system. Bartholomew Sikes was an excise officer whose method of measurement was the one adopted by the government in the Hydrometer Act of 1818. Spirit of proof strength is spirit which at 51 °F weighs exactly twelve-thirteenths of an equivalent amount of distilled water. Scales have been worked out to determine the proof gallonage at any temperature and at any strength.

From 1 January 1980 Britain is expected to adopt the system for measuring proof used by the majority of Common Market countries which belong to the International Organisation of Legal Metrology. The OIML system, which seems a much more logical one than the Sikes system, measures alcohol by percentage of volume at 20 °C, The comparative figures work out like this:

Sikes	OIML
70°	39.9%
75°	42.8%
80°	45.6%
100°	57.1%
120°	68.5%

Malt whiskies can be bought at 70, 80, 100 and 105° proof (Sikes); in other words they vary from about 40% alcohol to 60%, and as the duty increases by percentage volume of alcohol, so does the price.

Vatted malts

For those who find a single malt perhaps too distinct-ive, there are about twenty-five brands of vatted or blended malt on the market. None of them reveal their composition or the number of individual malts they contain, and I can't help feeling that one is taking a leap into the dark. Does mixing a powerful malt like Balmeanach with an equally prized malt like Glenlivet make something better than the sum of its parts, or something less?

The origin of 'vatting' lay in the practice of smooth-ing out differences in quality by mixing casks of differ-ent ages, but in the same distillery. From that it was a small step for blenders in Leith and Edinburgh to pro-cure parcels of malt and blend them to a saleable formula. There are some excellent vatted malts on the market today which appeal particularly to palates looking for marked flavour in their whisky and a symphony rather than a solo performance.

What is flavour?

And what is the special flavour of malt whisky that distinguishes it from other whiskies? A great deal of questionable piffle has been written, mainly by copy writers in advertising agencies, about the romance of malt whisky. As we've seen, an industry which sprung from illicit bothies in remote and picturesque places couldn't help but gather from the mists and the glens a most marketable image of genuine, rugged antiquity.

Were you to believe some of the copy, you might well think that all whisky was made by red-bearded, kilted Highlanders in heather-girt stills far from the madding world of Madison Avenue wordsmiths. The accent is on age, probity, tradition and quality. When Seagram were looking for a whisky which they could, without immodesty, describe in the glossy American magazines as 'the smoothest combination of all time' they went, according to the adman, to quite extra-ordinary lengths. The project took, it was claimed, a generation to perfect and the research involved nosing 530 distillations. Their blenders examined 'peat-tasting Scotches from the misty Isle of Islay, Scotches from Inverness as fragile as myrtle bloom. In one case we even had to buy a distillery to get a whisky we wanted.' So you can see that launching a new blend is not just throwing a few random casks together. The myrtle must be hunted, the distilleries snapped up!

When it comes to advertising their products, the adjectives most frequently used by the malt distillers are: mellow, smooth, well-rounded, soft, full-bodied, noble, mature, delicate, subtle, outstanding. Reference is frequently made to such enviable attributes as: distinction, tradition (generations of family distill-ing), the infinite care and patience which goes into the making of the product, and the fact that malt whisky is appreciated by 'connoisseurs.'

What is it that the connoisseurs find in malt whisky that can be found nowhere else? In many ways it is a liquor which defies analysis, consisting as it does of some two hundred or more compounds. An attempt is being made at the moment by scientists working at Pentland Scotch Whisky Research Ltd to establish a standard terminology for describing the aroma and flavour of whisky.

Up to now a large number of adjectives have been used to try to describe the differences between one malt and another. Words like: smoky, robust, peaty, clean, fragrant, fruity, woody, oily, honeyed, flowery, are frequently used. I have heard blenders themselves use more specific adjectives like: sharp, soapy, fatty, medicinal, washy (having the yeasty smell of wash), estery, solvency.

A whisky may well taste of rust if a nail or a piece of metal has found its way into the cask but, by and large, malt whiskies from individual distilleries, if properly matured and stored, tend to have a noticeable character which skilled blenders can recognise instantly. We'll consider blending a little more closely in a moment, but it's time we looked at the less romantic, far more commercial face of Scotch.

Grain whisky

Prepare to be disillusioned. Much of the whisky produced in Scotland is made not with malted barley in pot stills but almost entirely from maize in huge factory complexes.

Even at the beginning of the nineteenth century when labour was cheap and plentiful, men of action were looking for ways in which processes could be speeded up and the march of progress transformed into a gallop. Steamboats and steam trains were about to revolutionise travel in Scotland, and it was the careful control of steam that created the whisky industry we know today.

What distillers were looking for was a cheap device for producing spirit. The pot still, in which the mash had to be stewed and boiled and twice distilled, needed a great deal of skill and attention, and at the end of the process it yielded a whisky full of impurities which had to be eliminated or rectified if the spirit was to be exported to England for the making of gin.

The Lowland distillers relied heavily on the London market, and what they were looking for was a process which would give them as pure a spirit as possible. Several minds were at work. Robert Stein, a Lowland distiller, devised a continuous still which was tried out both in London and in Edinburgh in the late 1820's. Then Aeneas Coffey, Inspector General of the Excise in Ireland, devised an even more efficient still and he was granted a patent for it in 1831.

The advantage of the patent still was that it could be run twenty-four hours a day, seven days a week. No need for silent seasons, no need to clean out the still after each wash. The patent stills could be sited, as most of them are to this day, in towns because they did not rely on a constant supply of cold burn water.

In the early days of the patent still the mash was made of a mixture of malted and unmalted barley. The high tax on malt encouraged distillers to use as much unmalted barley as possible. When in 1846 the Corn Laws were repealed, imported maize was found to be a cheap and useful substitute for barley. In addition, maize was found to have a higher alcohol yield than barley. Small proportions of barley malt continued to be used to lend character to the spirit and, even more important, to carry out the chemical conversion of the starch in the maize into fermentable sugars.

The ascendancy of grain whisky

In the early days there was a very clear contrast between the product of the Highland pot still (the old-fashioned *uisge beatha*) and the new-fangled grain spirit produced in the economical Lowland patent stills. Less distinctive in taste, lighter in quality, grain whisky has often been referred to as a 'neutral spirit,' and indeed it is technically known as Plain British Spirit. Only when it has been matured in cask for a minimum of three years can it be termed Scotch grain whisky.

The battle between the mainly Highland malt distillers and the Lowland grain distillers was long and fierce. The malt distillers claimed that their product, made from Scottish barley, and possessed of a long and distinguished lineage and a recognisable flavour and quality, was the only product entitled to call itself 'Scotch whisky.' The outcome of the battle was to be decided by market forces.

In the mid-nineteenth century an Edinburgh whisky dealer called Andrew Usher made the discovery that malt whisky added to the cheaper grain spirit produced a blend which was eminently marketable. So marketable in fact, that today 95% of all Scotch whisky is sold as a blend of malt and grain.

It was not until 1909 that a government commission finally declared that the spirit 'distilled from a mash of cereal grains saccharified by the diastase of malt' and made in a patent still, was entitled to call itself *Scotch whisky* as long as it was distilled in Scotland. Move the patent still two feet across the border into England and it no longer produces Scotch.

Most of the grain distilleries operating in Scotland today use the Coffey still system in which two columns, an analyser and a rectifier strip the alcohol from the wash. But the very last word in grain distilleries has recently been completed overlooking the Clyde, in the old Gorbals district of Glasgow.

A grain distillery was built on the site in 1928, and indeed there was a malt distillery too, with two pot stills producing a Lowland malt called Kinclaith. Now the old malt distillery is gone and the new grain distillery, the largest in Europe, is in full production.

I flew back from Islay and Laphroaig, which has hardly changed in a hundred years, to look at the most modern manifestation of Scotch in the country. Strathclyde is a five-column distillation plant, producing 270,000 gallons of proof spirit a week. Most of it will mature as whisky; some will be sent down to Plymouth to be made into gin. A versatile plant indeed. It could even, according to the manager Michael Walker be programmed to produce malt whisky. The sort of presumption that would have had an old-fashioned Highland distiller reaching for his claymore!

'If we made up a mash based on barley then we could quite legally produce a product which we could describe as a Lowland malt whisky. Could we make Laphroaig here or Glenlivet? No most certainly not. We wouldn't be able to reproduce those characteristics at all.'

It is most unlikely that Strathclyde would ever wish to produce malt whisky; there is plenty around as it is but, the possibility is always there. The formula for making grain whisky currently uses yellow American maize, Finnish malt and soft Glasgow city water piped from Loch Katrine. The twenty-six washbacks use 1400 tons of maize and 100 tons of malt a week; the by-products are 450 tons of dark grains a week and fusel-oil which is sold to the manufacturers of perfume.

This is the side of the Scotch whisky industry that few people write about, but it is the silent, neutral backbone of famous blends that are sold with prose as purple as heather and as heady as myrtle. About 85 million gallons of grain whisky is produced in Scotland every year; about 67 million gallons of malt whisky. Neither could exist without the other, and in the blending lies the art and artistry of Scotland's great export.

The mixing of grain and malt

There could be up to thirty different malt whiskies in a blend; there may be several different grain whiskies too, it all depends on the supplies available and the market for which the blend has been created. Blenders are notoriously secretive about their activities; none of them will disclose their formulae, although if you spent enough time sniffing round their warehouses and noting the names on the casks you would have a good idea of what their blends contain.

It has been said that the mark of a good blender is his ability to know where to put his hands on a cask similar to the one he has not got. Because whisky may have to mature four, five or even more years before it is used, the ordering of whisky has to be done well in advance.

All the big companies make forecasts far into the future and they send their casks for filling all over Scotland. Naturally they draw most heavily on their own distilleries. So if you know what distilleries a blender owns then you have a shrewd idea of where quite a lot of his malt comes from. It's an exercise which wouldn't necessarily work with D.C.L., the company which holds the Scotch whisky jackpot. It owns forty-five malt distilleries and five grain distilleries and therefore has an enviable wealth of whisky to draw on for its market-leading brands: Abbot's Choice, Black & White, Dewar's, Crawfords's, Haig, John Parr, Vat 69, Johnnie Walker, King George IV, and the famous White Horse,

Once a company has found a successful blend which has popular appeal, it will take great pains to ensure that the taste remains unchanged from month to month and even from year to year. Reputable brands like Bell's, Standfast, Red Hackle, Spey Royal, Findlater's Finest, Long John, Highland Queen, Chivas Regal, Mackinlay's, Highland Cream, Queen Anne, Ballantine's, Whyte & Mackay's Special, all have their loyal following who are looking not for change but for the 'same again please!'

Changing tastes

In the postwar years there has been a move towards blends lighter both in flavour and in colour—a move dictated largely by the American market and the phenomenal success of Cutty Sark and J & B.

There are arcane reasons too why many whisky drinkers favour not a dark but a light-coloured whisky. Maurice Castle, the secret agent in Graham Greene's *The Human Factor* 'always bought J & B because of its colour—a large whisky and soda looked no stronger than a weak one of another brand.'

Although experts, who are nosing samples every day in their blending rooms, have a remarkable ability to distinguish one malt from another, and although many can identify the leading brands, the average drinker is far from expert. Blind tastings held from time to time have proved that even connoisseurs can be misled. De luxe whiskies are mistaken for inexpensive blends, and grain whisky confused with malt.

These days the average blend is 70% grain to 30% malt, although there are blends which use a higher or lower proportion of malt. Teacher's, which advertises itself as containing more malt whisky than other popular brands, is 50% malt, 50% grain. At its best the skill of blending lies in taking the whiskies when they are at their peak and marrying them so that the union is harmonious. Expediency often dictates that the blend is a compromise between what the blender would like to do and what market forces dictate.

The less you pay for a whisky, the less you will get in terms of quality. Good malt whisky costs money; poor malts which make poor blends come cheaper. Ideally a balance must be achieved between the heavier and lighter malts so that the constituent parts do not jar. Up to a certain point in time, the older the whisky the better. But the expensive 21 and 25-year-old blends are really self-defeating; few malt whiskies improve after fifteen years, and a blend which contains 25-year-old whiskies is likely to be no better than a blend half its age; the only remarkable thing about it would be the price. There are some excellent 'de luxe' blends on the market which do not state their age for the simple reason that, if an age is declared on a bottle then *every* whisky in the blend must be that age or older.

The technique of blending

Having fixed the formula—so many casks of this, so many casks of that—the next stage is to call the various whiskies into the blending hall where a sample from each cask is tested before it is emptied into a trough to mingle with the contents of other barrels.

When the whiskies are collected, usually in stainless steel tanks, they are aerated to encourage them to mix, and then often left to mature for a further period of up to eight months in wood. Many blenders return their whisky to casks for this period but one enterprising company, Waverley Vintners, recently decided that their Mackinlay whisky should be allowed to steep, not in cask, but in oak vats. A firm of coopers at Jarnac in the Armagnac country was commissioned to build eighteen vats, each holding 7900 gallons, which were then assembled in Leith; so now the Mackinlay blends will spend three months in French oak.

Just before bottling, the whisky is reduced by the addition of water to the required proof strength; it is then chilled and filtered to remove any substances that might cloud the golden liquid, especially if it were confronted with unusual temperatures in distant parts of the world. And then comes the bottling.

The proportions of the ideal blend are very much a matter of opinion. As one blender put it to me: 'If you're making up a blend you've got to decide what part of the market you're after—heavy, light or medium. And then you have to decide how you will compose your blend. So much of Islay, so much of Glenlivet, so much of North of Scotland and maybe the odd piece of Campbeltown or Orkney. And with a bit of luck you may hit it on the nose first time and everyone will say what a marvellous whisky. But of course you may be unlucky and people will say "My God what's this," and you've got to go back to the drawing board. But once you've got the blend right you stick with it, and in fact you become almost paranoiac about staying there.'

The difficulties of staying there are immense. As another blender put it: 'No two paper specifications for a blend will be alike. When the whiskies appear on the bench they may have come on a bit and you'll say "I'll only put in nine of those. These haven't come on quite so rapidly, I'll put in ten." Every time you look at the specification it's different. There's no question of pulling the yellowing formula out of the safe and telling the office boy to repeat the dose. So nobody can actually give you *the formula* of a blend.'

Enjoying Scotch

When it comes to Scotch there is an often confusing variety of choice. Sixty and more different malts to choose from, at varying degrees of strength and maturity. Two dozen or so vatted malts and several hundred different blends of malt and grain. By the way, if you are curious after all this talk of grain whisky, there is one unique brand on the market, Choice Old Cameron Brig, made by the Distillers Company at Cameronbridge in Fife where the earliest Stein still was erected. It is a well-matured and surprisingly pleasant whisky, surprising that is when one bears in mind the contempt in which the malt distillers have always held 'corn' whisky. There is no doubt that grain improves in wood but, lacking the frequently abundant compounds of malt, it takes a far shorter time to reach its peak and never achieves the wealth of flavour that is peculiar to the really great malts.

To dilute or not to dilute

A mild controversy occurred in the correspondence columns of a national paper recently on the merits and demerits of adulterating whisky with other fluids. Several enthusiasts seemed to be under the impression that most Scots took their dram neat from the bottle, and what was good enough for the Scots should be good enough for lesser breeds south of the border.

One distinguished English novelist and wine-writer claimed that since 'whisky came off the still' at 70° proof it would be a sacrilege to weaken it further. But, as we know, whisky comes off the still at various strengths. The middle cut which is selected by the stillman and diverted to the receiving tank starts running at 25 to 26° over proof, and it continues to be collected, depending on the practice of the individual distillery, down to 5° over proof. Before going to the warehouse the spirit, which probably has a strength somewhere between 15 and 25° over proof (between 115 and 125° proof Sikes), is reduced by the addition of spring water to between 11 and 12° over proof, and it is at this strength that it begins its three years and more mellowing in wood.

At the end of this period it is further reduced by the addition of water to the required strength. This may be 70, 80, 100, or 105° proof for a malt whisky, and usually 70° proof for blended whisky.

In an effort to counteract the crippling excise duty, there is a growing tendency to reduce some cheaper blends, intended for cut-price liquor stores, to 65.5° proof. These bargain whiskies are even less of a bargain if you remember that they are usually found in smaller than normal bottles, 70 centilitres not 75!

So whether you buy a 105° proof Glenfarclas single malt, a 100° proof Glencoe vatted malt, a 75° proof Chivas Regal blend or a 65.5° proof bottle of Auld Hielan' Grannie, you are getting a mixture of alcohol and water. How you further dilute it is entirely up to you.

Certainly if I were offered an outstanding malt whisky—a 15-year-old, 100° proof Glenlivet, say, or a 17-year-old 80° proof Macallan—I would like to appreciate it in the form in which it is offered. Just as you warm a fine brandy in the glass to release the aromas so you should nose a fine malt and savour its bouquet before, if you wish, bringing out its flavours even further by diluting it with no more than its own volume of water.

It is becoming increasingly popular to take a malt after a meal in place of cognac. Even then the pleasure is doubled, to my mind, by a restrained addition of water, especially if the malt is of high strength. The fragrance is there to be enjoyed both on the nose and in the mouth, and whisky should not enter the throat, as one keen Irishman observed of poteen, 'like a torchlight procession.' If you need fire in the belly try methylated spirits or paraffin.

What water?

If you live in a town where the water supply appears to come direct from the local swimming baths then it is advisable to use a bottled spring water. The fashion of drinking whisky-and-a-splash of soda has almost entirely died out. Sparkling mineral waters lend a texture to whisky which some enjoy, but I find the prickliness of added Perrier or Vichy interferes with the message the whisky carries—it's rather like reading a letter through frosted glass.

And talking of frost, should one ice the whisky or not? Again this is a question of choice. Few people would put ice cubes in a fine cognac or a fine malt, but on a hot day in a hot clime a blended whisky on the rocks has a lot to say for itself. In Scotland, for a large part of the year, the climate is bracing enough not to need qualifying with ice. And while we are on climate, I hope I will not incur the wrath of the whisky industry if I suggest that until you have tasted malt whisky diluted with the water from which it is made, in the country of its origin, you haven't fully appreciated it.

It is not that it doesn't travel well but it is peculiarly at its best when taken after a long day's exercise out on the hills or the moors. Neil Gunn, one of the many excisemen (Robbie Burns was another) who turned author, tells of the Englishman who had an inexhaustible knowledge of single whiskies and a proper regard for the right time to drink them.

One day Gunn was discussing the flavour of malts with him and he said 'Leaning against the wind and rain, you drive off from the first tee at Machrie. You feel your ball has gone straight, so with head down you plod on . . . Eighteen holes of that—and then a glass of Lagavulin! It's not that it revives you: it crawls along to your fingertips and toe-nails in a divine glow . . . But if I had been golfing at Eastbourne—would I have been looking forward to this potent stuff at the end?'*

Whisky cocktail and liqueurs

Enthusiasts with cocktail shakers have devised many ways of drinking Scotch. You can have it mixed in various proportions with such unlikely bedfellows as Cointreau, Crème de cacao, sherry, Bénédictine, gin, Pernod, vermouth.

To my mind whisky mixed with herbs and honey is an altogether more commendable venture. Drambuie, the biggest-selling liqueur in Britain and America, has a reputedly romantic past. The Mackinnons of Strath in the Isle of Skye who sheltered Prince Charles after his defeat at Culloden are said to have received from him, for the poor soul had little enough to give, a recipe for *an dram Buidheach*, 'a dram that satisfies.' The name Drambuie is a corruption of the Gaelic. Where the Prince got the recipe from is not revealed. The original success of Drambuie has brought competition in the shape of Glayva, Glen Mist, Clanrana and Lochan Ora, but Drambuie retains its lead in the market.

The most famous of all whisky concoctions is Atholl Brose which was used as a potent and secret weapon by a fifteenth-century Duke of Atholl. He overpowered his arch-enemy Ian Macdonald, the Earl of Ross and Lord of the Isles, by converting the well at which Macdonald frequently paused for refreshment into a font of whisky, honey and oatmeal.

Ideally you should use heather honey to make Atholl Brose and the recipe will be found on page 52.

* From *Whisky and Scotland*, Neil M. Gunn, Souvenir Press, 1977. Machrie golf course was laid out in 1891 on Islay. Today both it and its hotel are owned by Bowmore distillery which celebrated its bicentenary in 1979 so perhaps a glass of that excellent malt would be as appropriate as Lagavulin.

Whisky at the table

In the early days spirits were regarded in Scotland, as they were in the rest of Europe, more as a medicine than an everyday drink. Highland 'bitters' prepared by infusing whisky with spices and bitter herbs were taken on rising in the morning in much the same way that we might take a glass of liver salts. Even in the eighteenth century whisky was not a drink that would have appeared as the centrepiece of a gentleman's table.

When Boswell and Johnson visited the Highlands and Islands in 1773 they were offered claret, brandy, mountain from Malaga, frontignan from the South of France, porter and punch made of brandy or rum. When the future Lord Brougham visited the Western Isles at the end of the eighteenth century he recorded drinking claret, champagne, hermitage, hock and port ('Yesterday Campbell and I and two natives set in to it and among four had twelve port bottles and Bob being stowed away I finished another bottle and a half of port with an old exciseman'), but there was no mention of whisky.

There are several references in the memoirs of eighteenth- and early nineteenth-century travellers to the social distinctions of drinking. 'On going on board,' recorded Dr Thomas Garnett embarking for a day-trip to Staffa in 1798, 'we witnessed another proof of Mrs. Maclean's goodness, for we found *wine* for ourselves and *spirits* for the boatmen.'

Whisky was frequently mixed with milk and honey or sugar and melted butter to make a punch, but in all my reading I have come across no account of whisky being used in the preparation of more solid fare. Spirits were used to keep out the cold and warm the cockles of the heart, and when whisky was drunk it was considered sufficient sustenance in itself. In 1736 a traveller noted: 'the ruddy complexion, the nimbleness of these people is not owing to the water drinking but to the aqua vitae, a malt spirit which is commonly used both as victual and drink.'

As the nineteenth century waxed so did whisky production, and although the upper classes continued to pin their faith in claret and brandy, the lower orders took to whisky as readily as water. Lord Cockburn, the noted jurist and circuit judge, holding court at Tarbert on Monday, 17 September 1838, was particularly impressed by a worthy sempstress of Campbeltown who gave the court a detailed account of her habits:

'For above twenty-five years she has scarcely ever been in bed after five. The first thing she does after dressing is to go to a rock about a mile off and to take a large draught of water. She then proceeds about another mile in a different direction where she washes the taste of this out by a large draught of fresh water, after which she proceeds home and about half-past six puts on the tea kettle and breakfasts. This is a healthy and romantic seeming morning,' Cockburn concluded dryly, 'and therefore I regret to add that it was proved that three or four times a week the rest of the day is given to whisky.'

And not even given to creating splendid dishes with it as Dione Pattullo does in the pages that follow. I hope that the rest of this book will confirm what I have long suspected—there's more to enjoying Scotch than just pouring it in a glass.

Derek Cooper

Drinks

The art of mixing drinks is a very specialised one and in my opinion should be left in the hands of experts. However, many people like to experiment with mixing drinks, and the result can be some very weird and wonderful concoctions, some past description and only fit to pour down the drain; and many which go under names that are familiar but to which things have been added, again resulting in mixtures that bear little relationship to the originals. A great deal of the pain and misery, to say nothing of hangovers, can be avoided by reference to a good book or guide on the subject. Having had only a mild flirtation with the job of working in a cocktail bar, I decided to follow my own advice and went to the experts. As a result I got well briefed and have to thank the United Kingdom Bartenders Guild for the kind assistance rendered by Pat McCue of the Edinburgh Branch.

Whisky is a delicate drink and needs careful handling. There are many different flavours involved and some of the single malts have a completely different and distinctive flavour even to the complete novice. Some of them would be ruined by mixing with any other ingredients; and bearing in mind the price of the whisky itself, to say nothing of the skills of the makers and the blenders, it would be a shame to use them any other way than straight or with a little water. Blended whisky is a happier choice for mixing, and some of the light whiskys created for the American market can take more punishment of this sort than can some of the more malty and distinctive ones. It is as well to remember, too, that this spirit is not an all round mixer like gin or vodka, and attention should be paid to the basic flavours it mixes with. One thinks immediately of orange, but lemon goes well too. Pineapple was one of the surprises to me, but it seems a happy partnership.

Vermouths are widely used in whisky drinks and is a pleasant mix so long as the correct proportion is maintained. All the classic recipes have been tried and tried to obtain the right flavour, so stick to these and you won't go far wrong. A great standby are bitters of various kinds, and for the hot drinks honey is a pleasant sweetener for a change from sugar or sugar syrup.

My choice of recipes has been as wide as I could make it, and I hope covers most of the ways one can drink whisky. I have not tested them all myself, for had I done so in the short time I had to put this collection together, I should have been permanently half seas over and quite incapable of writing down a word. . . .

All the recipes collected here use a standard one-fifth of a gill measure. This will produce a three fluid ounce drink which should, if possible, be served in a cocktail glass. I have where possible, given the size and type of glass recommended, and it is wise to keep to this. Somehow the taste of the drink alters if it is served in a different shape glass, in the same way as china tea tastes delicious from fine porcelain but nothing out of thick pottery. Another point worth remembering is to chill the glasses beforehand if you have the facilities. Otherwise a quick swirl round with a few lumps of ice will help.

For the home mixer, a certain amount of basic equipment is required, and this short list might help to set you on your way. You will of course need glasses; various sizes crop up, but the choice of pattern is wide and sizes are standard. A mixing glass and glass rod with which to stir the contents, and what in the trade is called a hawthorn strainer to eliminate the etceteras not wanted in the glass. A shaker is required, and when using it for goodness sake shake it well—not a gentle rocking motion, but a good bang about.

A small board for cutting fruit and a stainless steel serrated bar knife. A bottle opener. A cork screw (often omitted). Ice bucket or thermos flask. A measure to ensure correct proportions. An ice crusher (or a tea towel and a hammer!). Some tooth picks and a lemon squeezer. Tongs for the ice. An ice lip water jug. A large bank account.

Dione Pattullo

Howtowdie Cocktail

1 measure Old Parr whisky
½ measure Van Der Hum
½ measure fresh orange juice
egg white
dash Grenadin
cherry

Put some ice in a shaker and add the whisky, Van Der Hum and the orange juice. Add some egg white and shake. Pour into a 3 oz cocktail glass and at this stage add a dash of Grenadin down the middle of the glass. Add the cherry on the stick and serve. This makes an eye catching and pleasant after dinner drink.

Scotch Corner

1 measure Old Parr Whisky
½ measure Van Der Hum
½ measure fresh lemon juice
dash Campari
twist of lemon

Put some ice in a shaker and add the whisky, Van Der Hum and lemon juice. Shake well and strain into a cocktail glass. Add the dash of Campari down the centre of the drink and add a twist of lemon. This produces a pretty pinky and dry mixture which is very refreshing.

*A selection of Scotch whiskies
(Courtesy of the Athenaeum Hotel, London, which offers
the finest selection of malt whiskies outside Scotland)*

Rusty Nail

Blood and Sand

1 measure whisky
1 measure Cherry Heering
1 measure orange juice

Put the ingredients into a mixing glass with plenty of ice and stir. Strain into a 3 oz cocktail glass.

Bobby Burns

1 measure whisky
1 measure sweet vermouth
3 dashes Bénédictine

Put some ice into a standard mixing glass and pour on the whisky, vermouth and Bénédictine. This quantity of Bénédictine is about half a teaspoon. Stir and then strain into a cocktail glass.

Ayrshire Relish

$\frac{1}{2}$ pint of fresh milk
2 measures whisky

Take a half pint of fresh Ayrshire milk and chill it. Stir in the whisky and serve at once.

Claude Mackay

1 measure whisky
1 measure Jamaica rum
½ measure Rose's lime juice

Put the ingredients with ice into a cocktail shaker.
Shake well and strain into a chilled cocktail glass.

Derby Fizz

1 teaspoon of icing sugar
1 teaspoon lemon juice
1 egg
3 dashes Orange Curaçao
1 measure whisky
soda water

In a shaker put the sugar, lemon juice, egg, Curaçao and
whisky. Shake and strain into a tumbler. Fill with soda
water.

Earthquake

1 measure gin
1 measure whisky
1 measure absinthe

Pour over ice in a mixing glass and stir. Serve in a chilled cocktail glass. This would produce an unquenchable glow—so go slow!

Flying Scotsman

3 measures whisky
2½ measures Italian vermouth
2 teaspoons Angostura bitters
2 teaspoons sugar syrup

Put ice into a mixing glass and pour in the whisky, vermouth and add the bitters and the syrup. Stir and strain into two 3 oz cocktail glasses. Makes 2

Silent Third

1 measure whisky
1 measure Cointreau
1 measure fresh lemon juice

Put ice into the shaker and add the whisky, Cointreau and lemon juice. Shake and then strain into a chilled 3 oz cocktail glass.

Wembley

1 measure whisky
1 measure dry vermouth
1 measure pineapple juice

Put the ingredients into a shaker with plenty of ice and shake well. Pour into a 3 oz cocktail glass and serve. This is a very feminine drink to be called after a place of such notable masculine orientation.

Whizz Bang

---

2 measures whisky
1 measure dry vermouth
2 dashes Pernod
2 dashes Grenadin
2 dashes orange bitters

In a mixing glass filled with ice stir the ingredients well. Strain into a cocktail glass . . . and wait for results. It is quite a mix!

Atholl Brose

---

oatmeal
heather honey
water
whisky

Stir equal quantities of meal and honey together with water to form a creamy consistency. Add a quantity of whisky and stir till it froths up. Lay it aside for two days to mature and strain into glasses to serve. If you cannot get the heather honey, a good substitute is the strong Hymetus honey from Greece.

Scotch Old Fashioned

Small lump sugar
3 dashes Angostura bitters
1 measure whisky
½ slice orange
cherry

Put the lump of sugar in the bottom of an Old Fashioned glass. Add the bitters and a little water to dissolve the sugar. Pour in the whisky and add a lump of ice, the orange and a cherry on a stick completing the picture.

Linstead

1 measure whisky
1 measure tinned pineapple juice
dash of Pernod
twist of lemon peel

In the shaker put some ice with the whisky, pineapple juice and the Pernod. Shake well and pour into a chilled cocktail glass. A twist of lemon peel completes this cloudy-looking but dryish cocktail.

Scotch Mist

1 measure whisky
crushed ice
twist of lemon
short straws

Fill an Old Fashioned glass with crushed ice. Pour the whisky over the ice and decorate with the twist of lemon. Stick the straws down the side and serve.

Hoots Mon

1 measure whisky
$\frac{1}{2}$ measure Lillet
$\frac{1}{2}$ measure sweet vermouth

In a mixing glass put some ice and then add the whisky, Lillet and the vermouth. Stir and then strain into a 3 oz cocktail glass. This drink has a soft whisky flavour owing to the addition of the Lillet.

Los Angeles

2 measures whisky
1 measure lemon juice
1 whole egg
dash of sweet vermouth

In the shaker put some ice and the rest of the ingredients. Shake very well and strain into a double cocktail glass, or any other 6 oz stemmed glass.

Summer Scotch

---

2 measures whisky
3 dashes white crème de menthe
ice
soda water

Put the ice and the whisky into a long 10 oz tumbler. Add the crème de menthe and fill up with soda water.

Barbican

7/10 whisky
1/10 Drambuie
2/10 passion fruit juice

If you use one teaspoon as a rough equivalent to 1/10 measure for this you will produce the right quantity for a 3 oz drink. The ingredients should be poured into an ice filled shaker and then shaken well. Strain into a chilled glass. This is a slightly sweet drink.

Whisky Cocktail

1 measure of whisky
1/5 of the measure Orange Curaçao
2 dashes of Angostura bitters
cherry

Have a mixing glass filled with lump ice and add the whisky, Orange Curaçao and the Angostura. Stir and strain into a 3 oz cocktail glass. Add the cherry and serve.

Suspension

1 measure Crabbie's Green Ginger Wine
1 measure whisky
1 measure orange squash

Put some ice into a mixing glass and add the ginger wine, the whisky and the undiluted orange squash. Mix well and serve with a cherry to give a glow to it.

The Gaslight

1½ measures whisky
1 measure Italian vermouth
dash bitters
1 teaspoon Drambuie

Put the ingredients into a mixing glass and stir well. Strain into a 3 oz cocktail glass.

Whisky Mac

I measure whisky
I measure Crabbie's Green Ginger Wine

Mix these two in a 3 oz glass or a small tub shaped glass.
This is the best thing I know for thawing out on a very
cold day after shooting or skating.

L. S. D.

I measure Drambuie
I measure whisky
I measure fresh lemon juice

Put all these into a shaker with some ice and shake well.
Strain into a 3 oz cocktail glass.

Mark Twain

I measure whisky
Juice of half a lemon
½ tablespoon sugar syrup
dash Angostura bitters
iced water

Put the whisky and the sugar into a tumbler and add the
bitters and strained lemon juice. Add ice if liked and fill
with iced water.

Prize Coo

1 pint warm milk
1 teaspoon honey
2 measures whisky

Warm the milk and sweeten with the honey. Add the whisky and drink from a hot glass. Some people might find this too sweet in which case a little lemon might be added.

Rob Roy

1 measure whisky
1 measure Italian vermouth
dash Angostura bitters

Put ice into a mixing glass and add the vermouth, whisky and the bitters. Stir before straining into a chilled 3 oz glass.

Rusty Nail

1 measure whisky
1 measure Drambuie

Mix these two in a glass and serve with caution. Malt whisky is preferable in this drink. *Illustrated opposite page 49.*

Hot Pint (a Traditional Hogmanay Drink)

1 quart Scotch pale ale
1 egg white
2 gills whisky
cloves
cinnamon
nutmeg

Bring the pale ale to the boil. Put the egg white and the whisky in a bowl and beat vigorously and while beating add a little of the hot ale. Now pour the whisky mix into the hot ale and add the cloves, cinnamon, and nutmeg to taste. Bring back to the boil and serve piping hot, maybe from a punch bowl, or in heatproof glass mugs.

Highland Coffee

To each cup of coffee add a $\frac{1}{2}$ measure of whisky, with sugar to taste. Pour some cream gently on to the top of the coffee using the back of a teaspoon to ensure its even spreading. Drink the coffee through the cream.

Highland Cooler

2 measures whisky
1 teaspoon sugar syrup
juice from half a lemon
2 dashes Angostura bitters
ice
ginger ale

In a 10 oz Highball glass put the syrup and lemon juice and the bitters. Add the whisky and the ice as liked. Top the glass up with ginger ale. Refreshing.

Highland Special

3 measures whisky
2 measures French vermouth
$\frac{1}{2}$ measure fresh orange juice

Pour the ingredients into a mixing glass with a little ice and stir. Strain over an ice cube into a 4 oz stemmed and chilled glass. Top with a dusting of grated nutmeg.

Hogmanannie

2 eggs
sugar
cream
1 gill whisky
ice

Separate the eggs and beat the yolks up with sugar and a little cream. Beat the whites separately. Stir the whisky into the yolks and then add the beaten whites. Stir before serving, with some caution. This bears the hallmarks of the hair of the dog!

Sabbath Morn

1 measure whisky
1 measure fresh cream
1 teaspoon heather honey

Put these ingredients into a glass and stir to mix. This will either set you up for the sermon or revive you after!

A Cordial of Currants

1 lb ripe white currants
$\frac{1}{4}$ oz ginger
2 lemons
1 quart whisky
1 lb lump sugar

Pick, wash and strip your white currants. Put them into a large jug with the grated ginger and the rind of the lemons. Add the whisky and cover. Allow this mix to stand for 24 hours before straining it through a hair sieve or a fine muslin cloth. Add a pound of lump sugar and stand for a further 12 hours. Pour into clean dry bottles using a metal funnel and cork closely. Delicious.

Scotch Horse's Neck

1 measure whisky
1 teaspoon lemon juice
dash of Angostura bitters
ginger ale

In a tumbler put some ice and add the whisky, juice and bitters. Fill up with ginger ale.

Scotch Rickey

1 measure whisky
juice of $\frac{1}{2}$ lime
juice of $\frac{1}{4}$ lemon
soda water

In a large glass put a lump of ice and to this add the juices and the whisky. Fill with soda water.

Stone Fence

2 oz whisky
ice
cider

Put the ice in a tall glass and add the whisky. Fill with cider to taste. This takes the sweetness of the cider and it becomes a very refreshing drink.

Whisky Collins

juice of $\frac{1}{2}$ lemon
2 oz whisky
dash bitters
1 teaspoon sugar syrup
soda water
lemon

In a 10 oz glass put some cracked ice with the juice of half a lemon. Add the sugar syrup and the whisky. Fill with soda water and add the bitters. Stir and serve with a slice of lemon.

Whisky Daisy

2 oz whisky
juice of $\frac{1}{2}$ lemon
6 dashes grenadin
mint
fruit
soda water

Fill the shaker with ice and pour in the whisky, juice and grenadin. Shake and strain into a goblet. Add some soda water and decorate with sprigs of fresh mint and slices of fruit in season. This could be apple, pear, orange or lemon.

Whisky Fix

1 teaspoon sugar
1 teaspoon water
juice of $\frac{1}{2}$ lemon
1 measure cherry brandy
2 measures whisky
ice
lemon

In a small tumbler put the sugar and water to dissolve. Add the juice of the lemon and the cherry brandy. Pour in the whisky and add ice to fill the glass. Stir gently and add the slice of lemon. Serve it with a straw. This should mix best with a malt whisky.

Whisky Flip

1 teaspoon sugar syrup
1 whole egg
2 oz whisky

Put these ingredients into a shaker with ice. Shake well and then strain into a 5 oz wine glass. Grate a little fresh nutmeg on top.

Whisky Highball

1 lump sugar
1½ measures whisky
ginger ale
orange slice

In a 10 oz tumbler put the sugar and whisky. Top up with ginger ale and float a slice of orange on top.

Whisky Sangaree

1 teaspoon sugar
2 measures water
2 measures whisky
crushed ice
nutmeg

In a small tumbler put the sugar and the water. Stir to dissolve and then add the whisky. Fill the glass with crushed ice and grate just a little nutmeg on the top. Serve with straws.

Whisky Sling

2 measures whisky
1 teaspoon sugar syrup
lump ice
water
slice of lemon

Mix the whisky and the sugar syrup. Add the ice and fill with water.

Whisky Smash

1 lump sugar
4 sprigs mint
little water
2 measures whisky
ice
orange slice
cherry
mint
lemon peel

Dissolve the sugar in a little water and add the mint sprigs. Crush these together. Add the ice and pour over the whisky. Decorate with a slice of orange and a cherry. Add a twist of lemon peel and a sprig of mint. Use an Old Fashioned glass for this drink.

Whisky Sour I

juice of $\frac{1}{2}$ lemon
$\frac{1}{2}$ teaspoon sugar
2 measures whisky
soda water
slice lemon

In a shaker full of ice put the lemon juice, sugar and whisky with a little of the soda water. Shake well and pour into an Old Fashioned glass. Add a slice of lemon before serving.

Whisky Sour 2

2 measures whisky
juice of ½ lemon
small teaspoon sugar syrup
white of egg
ice and soda water

Put the whisky, juice and sugar syrup into a shaker with a little egg white and ice. Shake well and pour over ice into an Old Fashioned glass. Top with soda water.

A Cold Whisky Punch

2 measures whisky
juice of ½ lemon
2 teaspoons sugar syrup
slices of orange

In a highball glass put the whisky and the lemon juice. Add the sugar syrup. Fill with iced water and top with slices of fresh orange.

Whisper

1 measure whisky
1 measure French vermouth
1 measure Italian vermouth
ice

In a mixing glass put ice and whisky with the two different vermouths. Serve over cracked ice in a stemmed glass.

Sherry Twist

$1\frac{1}{2}$ *measures sherry*
$\frac{1}{2}$ *measure whisky*
2 dashes Cointreau

Put these ingredients into a cocktail shaker with some ice. Shake well and pour into a double cocktail (5 oz) glass.

Thistle

---

1 measure whisky
1 measure sweet vermouth
1 dash Angostura bitters

Put the ingredients into a mixing glass with ice. Stir well and strain into a 3 oz cocktail glass.

Whisky Cobbler

---

2 measures whisky
1 teaspoon sugar syrup
4 dashes Curaçao
fruit

mint
straws

Put the whisky into a 7 oz glass and add the sugar syrup and Curaçao. Stir, add fruit and mint and sip through straws. Cooling for summer.

Whisky Zoom

---

1 teaspoon honey
1 teaspoon fresh cream
2 measures whisky

Dissolve the honey in a small basin with a very little boiling water. Pour into a shaker. Add the cream and the whisky and shake very well. Strain into a 3 oz cocktail glass.

The Best Medicine in the World

Honey mixed with whisky is a splendid and efficacious cure for the common cold. It also tastes very, very good!

Hot Whisky Toddy

1 teaspoon sugar
2 cloves
1 slice lemon
1 stick cinnamon
1½ measures whisky
boiling water

Take an Old Fashioned glass and put in the sugar, cloves, lemon slice and cinnamon. Stand a silver spoon in the glass and fill with boiling water. Stir to dissolve the sugar and drink as hot as possible.

A Hot Toddy

1 good measure whisky
1 teaspoon sugar or more to taste
1 slice lemon
a spoonful of honey
boiling water

Into a heatproof glass put the whisky and add a quantity of boiling water. Stir in the sugar and the honey. Top with a slice of lemon. If you do not have a heatproof tumbler for this, use a silver spoon standing in the glass to help prevent the glass cracking.

Round the World

1 measure Bols banana liqueur
½ measure whisky
dash Cointreau
dash of orange squash
mandarin slice
ice

In a mixing glass put the banana liqueur and the whisky with plenty of ice. Add the dash of Cointreau and the undiluted orange squash. Stir and strain into a cocktail glass. Add the mandarin and serve.

Whisky Recipes

Cooking with whisky is not one of the most obvious things to do with this excellent spirit, and in truth it is only in the last 20 years that it has taken the fancy of the cook or chef who likes to make experimental forays into the unknown. Many of the results have been unexpectedly good, and some have even become classics in this short space of time. Lobster with whisky, for instance, is one of the nicest ways of presenting this delicacy. Use whisky, too, in sauces for crayfish, scampi, scallops and crab. Most shellfish, in fact, react favourably with whisky.

Not surprisingly, perhaps, whisky enhances the flavour of game birds, in particular the otherwise rather tasteless pheasant, and pigeons, quails and guinea fowl. Whisky with beef, whisky with pork, whisky in the marinade for game pies and pâtés—whisky adds lustre to the dishes in which it is incorporated.

Sweet dishes tend to react differently to the flavour of whisky and need a different type of approach. Whisky goes particularly well with oranges and with coffee-flavoured creams and cakes. One of my own favourites is the jelly made with green ginger wine and whisky, topped lavishly with sweetened whipped cream. It is a dessert that is particularly pleasing to men and has had considerable success with those who don't eat puddings.

It is necessary to note the distinction between different whiskies for cooking. As far as is possible, I have given my preference in the recipe instructions. On the whole the puddings and sweet dishes are best made with a single malt, but in the making of savoury sauces it is a waste to use an expensive malt when a blend will do just as well. Almost all the recipes I have tried with both kinds of whisky, except where commonsense dictated otherwise. I have eaten everything in the book, and I know it all works in the quantities given. Adventurous cooks may wish to try other proportions, but I should counsel against adding too much extra whisky, for it can kill the flavour of some of the dishes, or can send your guests home wondering what hit them. The recipes are designed to feed 4-6 persons unless stated otherwise. At this juncture, it is needful for me to thank all my friends who became guinea-pigs for the second trials of the dishes, and to my children for suffering the successes and the failures of the initial tests. This book has been the greatest of fun to produce, and I hope it will give inspiration to those who wish to try something a bit different.

A special thanks, too, to the Mushroom Growers Association who provided me with the recipe and the photograph of the Scotch Marinaded Mushrooms opposite page 81.

Dione Pattullo

Starters

Scotch Marinaded Mushrooms

2 tablespoons whisky
3 tablespoons oil
2 teaspoons lemon juice
$\frac{1}{2}$ level teaspoon fresh thyme
2 level teaspoons chopped parsley
$\frac{1}{4}$ level teaspoon castor sugar
salt and pepper
100 g (4 oz) button mushrooms, washed and dried

Mix together the ingredients, except the mushrooms. Stir well to blend. Put into a container with a lid, add the mushrooms and put on the lid. Turn to coat the mushrooms with the liquid and leave to stand for about 2 hours. Turn the container frequently to toss the mushrooms in the marinade regularly during this time. Serve the mushrooms with a little of the marinade and with fresh crusty bread and butter. *Illustrated opposite page 81.*

Highland Mushroom Savoury

25 g (1 oz) butter
200 g (8 oz) button mushrooms, quartered

50 ml (1/8 pint) whisky
½ oz stem ginger, cut into small dice
100 ml (¼ pint) single cream
I level tablespoon cornflour
salt and pepper

Melt the butter and lightly sauté the mushrooms. When just tender, stir in the whisky and ginger. Blend the cream with the cornflour, and stir into the mixture. Stir until thickened. Season to taste and serve on toast rounds or fried bread. Sprinkle with chopped parsley.

Scotch Mushroom Cocktail

150 g (6 oz) clean mushrooms
I small lettuce, washed and shredded
30 ml (2 tablespoons) cream
30 ml (2 tablespoons) mayonnaise or salad cream
15 ml (I tablespoon) tomato ketchup
I teaspoon blended whisky
¼ teaspoon Worcester sauce
salt and black pepper

Wipe the mushrooms and peel only if the stems are discoloured. Slice very thinly using a stainless steel knife. Wash and shred the lettuce or as much as you need to line 4 ramekins. Half whip the cream and blend in the mayonnaise, sauce, ketchup and whisky. Season with salt and freshly ground black pepper to taste. Fold in the mushrooms. Divide between the ramekins and serve with a dusting of finely chopped parsley.

Pâté Maison

1 onion
15 g (½ oz) butter
200 g (8 oz) calf liver
100 g (4 oz) pie veal
100 g (4 oz) salt pork
30 ml (1 fl oz) malt whisky
25 ml (1½ tablespoons) flour
salt
¾ teaspoon black pepper
pinch thyme
pinch nutmeg

Chop the onion very finely. In a sauté pan melt the butter and brown the onion very slowly. Mince the meats with the onion three times. Blend in the flour, whisky and the seasonings and herbs. Butter a 6-inch terrine and put the mix into this. Stand the terrine in a dish with one inch of water in it. Bake covered at 250 °F, Gas 2, for 2 hours. Cool. Run some clarified butter over the top to seal if it is not to be used at once. Keep in fridge.

Shrimp Pâté

200 g (8 oz) shrimps
1 teaspoon malt whisky
30 ml (2 tablespoons) lemon juice
rind of ½ lemon
3 leaves dill
1 teaspoon black pepper
¼ teaspoon mace
salt to taste
45 ml (3 tablespoons) oil

Mince the shrimps finely and blend in the whisky, lemon juice and finely grated lemon rind, the chopped dill and the rest of the seasonings. Add the oil gradually and beat until creamy. Put into small containers and cover with clarified butter. Chill. Serve with hot toast or fairy toast.

Crab Soup

1 medium cooked crab
600 ml (1½ pints) good chicken stock
anchovy essence
pepper
mace
200 ml (½ pint) cream
30 ml (2 tablespoons) blended whisky
paprika

Shred the crab meat finely. Heat the chicken stock and warm the cream. Season the stock with pepper and mace. Add the crab and heat gently. Add anchovy essence to taste, about 1 teaspoon. Stir in the cream and whisky. Now check for salt, remembering the anchovy is salty. Add salt or essence only if required. Serve hot with a sprinkling of paprika.

Fish

Fish Mousse Mackinlay

$\frac{1}{2}$ kg (1 lb) flounder or plaice fillets
200 ml ($\frac{1}{2}$ pint) milk
2 eggs
30 ml (2 tablespoons) potato flour
$\frac{1}{4}$ teaspoon nutmeg
50 ml ($\frac{1}{4}$ gill) milk
50 ml ($\frac{1}{4}$ gill) whisky
200 ml ($\frac{1}{2}$ pint) double cream
lobster meat for garnish

Cut the fish into small pieces and put in a blender with 200 ml ($\frac{1}{2}$ pint) milk, eggs and potato flour. Cover and blend at a high speed for 2 minutes. Remove the cover and pour in slowly the milk, whisky, nutmeg and cream. When blended turn off the machine and turn into a well-buttered two-pint mould. Set in a pan of hot water and bake in a moderate oven (350 °F, Gas 4, 160 °C) for 1 hour or until the middle is set. Unmould and garnish with the lobster. Serve with a sour cream sauce. *Illustrated opposite page 96.*

Turbot Kinloch

fish stock
1 kg (2 lb) turbot steaks
50 g (2 oz) butter
1 onion minced
150 g (12 oz) tomatoes

100 g (4 oz) prawns
45 ml (3 tablespoons) whisky
salt, pepper and sugar
parsley

Make a good fish stock, well flavoured with lemon, mace and peppercorns. Strain into a clean shallow pan. Poach fish steaks gently for 5–6 minutes. Melt 50 g (2 oz) butter and in it gently sauté the onion. When soft add the chopped tomatoes. Simmer for 10 minutes. Add salt, pepper and sugar to taste. Add a gill of stock if needed to prevent it drying out. Finally add the prawns and the whisky. Simmer for a few minutes more and pour over the dished fish. Garnish with parsley.

Fillet of Sole

1 kg (2 lb) filleted sole
20 ml (2 tablespoons) diced shallot
1 crushed clove of garlic
50 g (2 oz) butter
2 tomatoes, chopped
200 g (8 oz) mushrooms
35 g (1½ oz) flour
60 ml (2 fl oz) blended whisky
200 ml (½ pint) cream
1 can artichoke hearts

Butter a sole dish and lay the fillets of sole in it, folded in half. Sauté the chopped shallot and garlic in half the butter and when brown add the chopped tomatoes. Continue to cook until soft and then sieve the sauce. Sauté the washed and sliced mushrooms in the rest of the butter. Stir the flour and whisky into the sieved onion mix and cook gently for 3–4 minutes without browning. Warm the cream and add to the onion mix.

Cook until it thickens slightly. Add the mushrooms and a little of the liquor from the can of artichokes. Pour the sauce over the fish and bake at 400 °F, Gas 6, 200 °C for 15 minutes. Heat the artichokes in a pan in the remaining liquor. Drain them and use to garnish the dish of sole with some added parsley sprigs.

Loch Leven Trout

3 medium brown or rainbow trout
seasoned flour
35 g (1½ oz) butter
50 g (2 oz) flaked browned almonds
45 ml (3 tablespoons) whisky
lemon

Toss the cleaned fish in seasoned flour. Melt the butter and when it is frothing put in the fish. Cook for 5 minutes on each side. Add the almonds and toss lightly until hot. Pour in the whisky and flame, shaking the pan until the flame dies. Add a squeeze of lemon juice to taste and serve very hot with lemon wedges. Serves 3. *Illustrated opposite.*

Whisky'd Scallops

6 scallops
¼ cup water
30 ml (2 tablespoons) blended whisky
1 small onion
10 g (½ oz) butter

Loch Leven Trout, Mushroom and Veal Kidney Vol au Vent, Whisky Drops

Scotch Marinaded Mushrooms
(Courtesy of the Mushroom Grower's Association)

6 medium mushrooms, minced
15 ml (1 tablespoon) flour
salt and pepper
lemon juice
mashed potato

Clean the scallops and put in a small pan with water and whisky. Simmer for 6–8 minutes. Chop the onion and sauté in the butter. Add the mushrooms and cook a minute or two. Add the flour and stir over heat until the flour bursts and thickens. Stir in the cooking liquor from the fish and boil until thick. Season with salt, pepper and lemon juice to taste. Pipe a border of mashed potato on the shells. Put the fish in the sauce and divide between shells. Grill to brown the potato. Serve at once.

Crab and Mushroom Scallops

100 g (4 oz) mushrooms, peeled and sliced
25 g (1 oz) butter
salt, pepper and cayenne
200 ml ($\frac{1}{2}$ pint) béchamel sauce
15 ml (1 tablespoon) whisky
150 g (6 oz) white crab meat
dry breadcrumbs

Sauté the mushrooms in the butter. Season the sauce to taste. Add the mushrooms and whisky with flaked crab meat and stir in. Divide between 6 buttered scallop shells. Sprinkle with freshly browned breadcrumbs. Dot with butter and reheat in a hot oven (450 °F, Gas 7, 220 °C) for 6–8 minutes. Serve at once.

Lobster with Whisky Sauce

2 boiled lobsters
25 g (1 tablespoon) butter
25 g (1 oz) flour
200 ml ($\frac{1}{2}$ pint) lobster or fish stock
100 ml ($\frac{1}{2}$ cup) sour cream
50 ml ($\frac{1}{4}$ cup) malt whisky
15 ml (1 tablespoon) chopped fresh dill
boiled rice
paprika

Split the lobsters down the back with a sharp knife and put the bones in a pan with sole bones if available, a bay leaf and a piece of mace. Boil for 20 minutes only, then strain to give $\frac{1}{2}$ pint stock. Make a sauce by melting the butter, adding flour and stock. Boil for 3 minutes stirring all the time. Whisk in the sour cream and whisky. Chop the lobster meat into 1 inch pieces and the dill finely. Add to the sauce and reheat gently. Serve in a ring of plain boiled rice and sprinkle with paprika.

Main Dishes

Beef Casserole

800 g (2 lb) shin of beef
1 cup malt whisky
30 ml (2 tablespoons) chopped parsley
1 teaspoon thyme
1 bay leaf
1 sliced onion
100 g (4 oz) fat bacon
2 tablespoons olive oil
15 ml (1 tablespoon) flour
½ pint stock
seasoning

Cut the shin of beef into 1–1½ inch cubes. Mix the whisky, parsley, thyme, bay and onion in a bowl and add the meat. Marinate in this mix, turning the meat as often as possible, for about 4–6 hours or overnight. Chop the fat bacon and add to a casserole in which you have put 2 tablespoons olive oil. Heat gently until the fat of the bacon runs. Take the meat out of its marinade and toss in the flour. Brown the meat on all sides very slowly. Add the rest of the marinade and season with salt and pepper. Add stock to just cover and put in a low oven (325 °F, Gas 3, 160 °C) and cook for about 3 hours.

Hunter's Steak

250 g (10 oz) steak
25 g (1 oz) butter
15 ml (1 tablespoon) minced onion
15 ml (1 tablespoon) malt whisky
salt and pepper
tabasco

Beat the steak very thin. Heat half the butter and brown steak quickly on both sides. Add the onion and brown lightly. Add the whisky and set alight. When flame goes out add rest of the butter. Season to taste. Add a few drops of tabasco and simmer gently for 4–5 minutes. Serves 1.

Veal Chop Faskelly

25 g (1 oz) butter
4 veal chops
1 onion, minced
50 g (2 oz) mushrooms
1 tablespoon tomato purée
50 ml ($\frac{1}{2}$ gill) stock
30 ml (2 tablespoons) whisky

Melt the butter in a skillet. Brown the veal on both sides for 2–3 minutes. Add the minced onion and continue cooking over a moderate heat until the onion is brown. Add the mushrooms and cook gently for 2–3 minutes. Mix the tomato purée and stock. Add the whisky to the meat and flame it. When the flame dies, add the stock. Put the lid on and allow to cook gently for about 10 minutes. Sprinkle with chopped parsley.

Veal, Ham and Prune Loaf

1 kg (2 lb) veal
$\frac{1}{2}$ kg (1 lb) ham
1 onion
1 clove garlic
6 juniper berries
12 prunes
$\frac{1}{2}$ cup whisky
bay leaf
thyme
marjoram
4 eggs
3 cups porridge oats
1 tablespoon Worcester sauce
2 teaspoons anchovy essence
salt
black pepper
streaky bacon
$\frac{1}{2}$ kg (1 lb) sausagemeat

Mince the veal and ham together with onion and garlic.
Add juniper berries and mince. Soak prunes overnight
and cook in whisky. Crumble herbs if dried or chop
finely if fresh. Mix minced meats with eggs, porridge
oats, Worcester sauce and anchovy essence. Season
with some salt and a little freshly ground black pepper.
Add the whisky from the prunes. Line a loaf tin with
strips of streaky bacon. Put in half the mix. Layer with
the sausagemeat in a long strip. De-stone prunes and
lay down the middle. Top with rest of the mix. Cover
with more bacon and set in a dish of water. Bake for
$1\frac{1}{2}$–2 hours in a moderate oven.

Mushroom & Veal Kidney Vol au Vent

1 x 6-inch vol au vent case cooked
4 veal kidneys
salt and pepper
25 g (1 oz) butter
100 g (4 oz) mushrooms
30 ml (2 tablespoons) whisky
200 ml (½ pint) veal stock
10 ml (2 teaspoons) potato flour

Skin and slice the veal kidneys. Season with salt and pepper. Melt the butter in a sauté pan and cook the kidney in this over a high flame for 5 minutes. Take the kidneys out with a slotted spoon. Quarter the mushrooms and add them to the fat. Cook gently until soft and return the kidneys to the pan. Pour in the whisky and set alight. When the flare dies stir in most of the stock. Mix the potato flour with a little stock and add to the pan. Cook until the sauce is thick. Keep warm. Take lid off vol au vent case and scoop out any excess pastry. Fill the hot mix into the case and serve at once. *Illustrated opposite page 80.*

Lamb Noisettes

6 noisettes of Scotch Lamb
cut clove of garlic
salt and pepper
50 g (2 oz) butter
30 ml (2 tablespoons) malt whisky

6 fried croûtons, approximately the size of the noisettes
100 ml (¼ pint) cream
artichoke hearts
duchesse potatoes

Ask your butcher to tie the noisettes unstuffed. Rub
each side with the cut clove of garlic and then season
with salt and pepper. Melt the butter in a heavy frying
pan and brown the noisettes on both sides. Continue
to sauté until cooked through. Fry the croûtons in a
separate pan. Pour the whisky over the noisettes and
flame. Stir in the cream scraping the sides and bottom
of the pan and blending in any juices. Adjust seasoning.
Put the noisettes on the croûtons, pour over the sauce
and serve with duchesse potatoes and the heated artichoke hearts.

Stuffed Fillet of Pork

18–20 prunes
30 ml (2 tablespoons) malt whisky
90 ml (6 tablespoons) water
whole almonds
100 g (4 oz) butter
2 whole pork fillets
2 minced onions
1 minced clove garlic
salt and pepper
30 ml (2 tablespoons) malt whisky
200 ml (½ pint) stock
potato flour

Cook the prunes in the whisky and water until soft. Split and remove the stones. Fill each prune with a whole almond in its place. Using a very thin bladed sharp knife poke a hole down the centre of each fillet. Stuff the prunes down the hole so provided. This is not as hard as it sounds as it goes with the grain of the meat. Melt the butter in a skillet with a lid. Sauté the fillets until browned on all sides. Add the onion and garlic and seasoning, and sauté for a few minutes until transparent. Pour in 2 tablespoons whisky, stock and liquor over from prunes. Cover and simmer for 40 minutes. Strain off the sauce and thicken with potato flour. Cut fillets on a slant in slices about half an inch thick. Pour over the seasoned sauce and serve hot.

Kidney Nicole

1 kidney
10 g ($\frac{1}{2}$ oz) butter
5 ml (1 teaspoon) chopped onion
1 small rasher of bacon
2 medium mushrooms, sliced
1 tomato
5 ml (1 teaspoon) whisky
1 drop Angostura bitters
salt and pepper

Peel, split and slice the kidney. Melt the butter and sauté the kidney for 2 minutes. Add the onion and bacon in strips. Cook until slightly browned. Put the mushrooms in with roughly chopped tomato. Cook until the tomato is soft. Add the whisky, bitters and salt and pepper to taste. Serve very hot with plain boiled rice. Serves 1.

Tongue in Caledonia Sauce

25 g (2 tablespoons) raisins
30 ml (2 tablespoons) whisky
1 large onion, chopped
25 g (2 oz) butter
25 g (2 oz) flour
1 tin concentrated consommé
½ teaspoon fresh mustard
100 ml (¼ pint) tinned tomatoes
salt and pepper
300 g (12 oz) cooked fresh tongue in thick slices
chopped parsley

Soak the raisins in the whisky for 2 hours. Sauté the chopped onion in the butter and add the flour. Brown well. Make the consommé up to ¾ pint with water and add to the flour mix, with mustard, tomatoes and seasoning. Boil for 5 minutes stirring occasionally. Put a layer of sauce in an ovenproof dish. Lay on the meat cut in slices. Mix the raisins and whisky with the rest of the sauce. Bring to the boil again. Pour over the meat and put in a moderate oven (350 °F, Gas 4, 180 °C) for 5–10 minutes. Garnish with parsley.

Chicken Beaulieu

6–8 chicken joints
salt and pepper
30 g (1½ oz) butter
2 rashers streaky bacon
¼ cup carrots cut in matchsticks
1 tablespoon chopped onion
25 g (1 oz) butter

$1\frac{1}{2}$ cups stock
45 ml (3 tablespoons) blended whisky
potato balls

Season the chicken joints with salt and pepper and brush with melted butter. Bake in a casserole at 375 °F, Gas 5, 190 °C for 12–15 minutes. Cut the bacon in strips and put in a sauté pan. Cut the carrots in matchsticks and boil in salted water for 5 minutes. Drain. Sauté the chopped onion in the bacon fat, adding butter if needed. When just browning add the carrots and fry 2–3 minutes. Add stock and bring to the boil. Add the whisky and pour over the chicken joints. Check seasoning and cover. Bake at 350 °F, Gas 4 180 °C for 35 minutes. Add potato cut with a melon baller and cook until they are tender. Serve at once.

Chicken and Scampi Cardean

$1\frac{1}{2}$ kg ($3\frac{1}{2}$ lb) chicken
400 ml (1 pint) water
salt and pepper
2 sticks celery
150 g (10 oz) rice
1 onion, minced
50 g (2 oz) butter
1 teaspoon potato flour
3 ml (2 tablespoons) Harvey's sauce
few drops Worcester sauce
400 ml (1 pint) chicken stock
30 ml (2 tablespoons) whisky
200 g ($\frac{1}{2}$ lb) scampi
parsley

Set the chicken in a deep casserole with water, seasoning and celery. Bake in a moderate oven (350 °F, Gas 4, 180 °C) for 1½ hours. Strain off the stock and in it boil the rice for 12 minutes. Take the flesh off the chicken bones. Drain the rice and wash under a running tap. Sauté the onion in butter until just beginning to brown. Add the rice. Cook until brown and keep hot. Mix the potato flour with Harvey's and Worcester sauces, and some cold water if needed. Mix with 1 pint of chicken stock and seasoning. Add the whisky. Place the chicken pieces and scampi in a shallow casserole, pour over the sauce and heat for 20 minutes in a moderately hot oven (375 °F, Gas 5, 190 °C). Dish with the rice in the middle and the chicken and scampi all round. Mince parsley over the rice for colour. Serves 8.

Duck with Orange and Whisky and Olives

1 duckling
1 orange
12–18 stoned olives
1 tablespoon whisky
salt and pepper

Prepare the duck by stuffing ½ orange in the cavity. Rub the bird's skin with the other half and sprinkle with salt. Roast on a rack at 375 °F, Gas 6, 180 °C for 1½ hours. Warm the olives in the whisky. Drain off the duck fat and baste with the whisky and olives 30 minutes before serving. Dish the duck and make a gravy with the duck dripping and whisky and some stock made from the giblets. Pour round the bird with the olives. Serve with mashed potato.

Ladywell Pie

1 rabbit, jointed
300 g ($\frac{3}{4}$ lb) salt belly of pork
300 g ($\frac{3}{4}$ lb) puff or flaky pastry

Forcemeat
rabbit liver
50 g (2 oz) fat bacon
50 g (2 oz) breadcrumbs
thyme
parsley
nutmeg
egg to bind

Sauce
1 large onion, minced
15 ml (1 tablespoon) flour
200 ml ($\frac{1}{2}$ pint) brown stock
salt and pepper
50 ml ($\frac{1}{2}$ gill) Mackinlays whisky

Soak the rabbit joints in cold water for 1 hour. To make the forcemeat, mince the liver and bacon, and add to them the rest of the forcemeat ingredients, reserving a little egg. Form into balls about 1 inch in diameter. Dice the salt pork and put into a heavy pan until the fat runs and the meat is crisp. Take out with a draining spoon. Put the rabbit, pork and forcemeat balls into a pie dish. For the sauce, brown the minced onion in some of the pork fat and add the flour and stock. Cook until thick. Season with salt and pepper, and add the whisky. Pour over the meats in the pie dish. Roll out the pastry to fit, put on the pastry lid and decorate. Brush with rest of egg and bake at 400 °F, Gas 6, 200 °C for 1–1$\frac{1}{2}$ hours.

Rabbit Terrine

1 large rabbit, jointed
30 ml (2 tablespoons) oil
15 ml (1 tablespoon) whisky
15 ml (1 tablespoon) dry vermouth
bay leaf
clove garlic
12 peppercorns
200 g (8 oz) chicken livers
salt and pepper
100 g (4 oz) bacon rashers
200 g (8 oz) sausagemeat

Take the meat off the rabbit bones. Mix oil, whisky and vermouth and add bay, garlic and peppercorns. Add the meat and stand covered overnight. Clean the chicken livers and season with salt and pepper. Line a loaf tin with bacon rashers and put in a layer of rabbit, then a layer of livers and then the sausagemeat. Fill up with the rest in the same mode. Pour the marinade through a sieve over the terrine. Bake at 350 °F, Gas 4, 180 °C for 1½ hours. Cool and chill. Serve in slices with salad, or with toast and butter.

Raisin Stuffed Pigeons

4 pigeons
50 g (2 oz) raisins
30 ml (2 tablespoons) water
15 ml (1 tablespoon) whisky

8 slices of bacon
75 g (3 oz) butter
100 g (4 oz) mushrooms
salt and pepper
stock

Bone off the breasts of the pigeons and beat with a meat hammer to break down tough fibres. Boil the raisins in the water and whisky for 2–3 minutes. Divide raisins between the breasts and roll each one up. Wrap a slice of bacon round each and secure with a toothpick. Melt butter in a casserole and put in the pigeons. Baste and allow to cook uncovered for 30 minutes at 375 °F, Gas 5, 190 °C. Add stock and seasoning. Put on the lid and return to a slow oven (325 °F, Gas 3, 160 °C) for 1 hour. Quarter the mushrooms and add them. Cook for a further 30 minutes. Thicken the sauce with potato flour broken with a little cold water. Serve with mashed potato.

Grilled Guinea Fowl

2 guinea fowls
juice of 1 orange
2 tablespoons whisky
4 tablespoons olive oil
1 bay leaf
fresh ground black pepper
salt

Split the guinea fowls or take off the bones in joints. Mix the rest of the ingredients and whisk together. Put the joints in the mixture and allow to marinate for at least 6 hours, or overnight. Pat dry and put under a medium grill. Brush with the marinade if too dry. Turn the joints half way through the cooking period.

Stuffed Quails

50 g (2 oz) raisins
30 ml (2 tablespoons) whisky
30 ml (2 tablespoons) water
2 cloves
1 onion
100 g (4 oz) butter
½ cup cooked rice
50 g (2 oz) walnuts
juice of 1 orange and 5 ml (1 teaspoon) orange rind
6 boned quails
6 large slices of bacon
200 ml (1 pint) stock
salt and pepper
1 teaspoon potato flour

Put raisins in whisky with water and cloves. Simmer for 2–3 minutes and leave to swell. Take out the cloves. Strain. Keep the liquor. Sauté 1 tablespoon onion in ½ oz of butter and add. Mix the fruit with the rice and finely chopped walnuts. Add the orange rind and 1 oz melted butter. Stuff into quails. Coat each with some butter and wrap in bacon. Make stock with quail bones or use good chicken stock. Season well. Roast the quails for 5 minutes at 450 °F, Gas 8, 225 °C and then turn heat down to 300 °F, Gas 2, 150 °C. Baste with orange juice and liquor from fruit and some stock. Cover and cook a further 20 minutes. Thicken sauce with potato flour and serve at once.

Scotch Mushrooms and Whisky Sauce

4 large open mushrooms or 8 small ones
25 g (1 oz) butter
600 g (1½ lb) sausage meat
1 egg
breadcrumbs
deep fat for frying

Cook mushrooms in butter for 3–4 minutes. Season with salt and freshly ground black pepper. Cover with sausage meat sealing all holes. Dip in flour, beaten egg and finally breadcrumbs. Repeat if liked. Fry in deep fat until golden brown. Serve with the following whisky sauce:

Whisky Sauce
1 carrot
1 onion
small piece turnip
25 g (1 oz) butter
25 g (1 oz) flour
½ pint stock or water
salt and pepper
parsley, thyme and bay leaf
mushroom ketchup
½ gill whisky

Fish Mousse Mackinlay

Prunes in Whisky Jelly (above), Whiskied Oranges (below)

Prepare and slice the vegetables and cook them gently in the fat until they are golden brown. Add flour and cook for a further 5–10 minutes. Blend in stock and add salt and pepper. Add herbs tied in a piece of butter muslin and also about a tablespoon of mushroom ketchup, or to taste. Simmer gently for about 30 minutes. Strain and reduce by further boiling if necessary. Add whisky and allow to boil for a moment more, and then check the seasoning. (Also very good with grilled steaks.)

Pentland Potato

4–6 potatoes
10 g ($\frac{1}{2}$ oz) butter
salt and pepper
100 ml ($\frac{1}{4}$ cup) cream
15 ml (1 tablespoon) whisky

Peel and boil the potatoes in salted water. Drain and put back on heat to dry well. Force through a potato ricer. Add butter, salt and pepper. Beat in the cream and then the whisky. Beat until smooth and light over a low heat to reheat. Serve with a stew with lots of vegetables in it.

Sweets

Banana Royal

6 bananas
3 eggs, separated
3 dessertspoons sugar
15 ml (1 tablespoon) whisky

Mash the fruit with a stainless steel fork. Beat the egg yolks and sugar until light. Mix in the bananas and then fold in the stiffly beaten whites and the whisky. Put into a pretty dish and refrigerate for a short while. Serve immediately, as this dish might separate if kept.

Baked Whisky Oranges

6 oranges
30 ml (2 tablespoons) butter
30 ml (2 tablespoons) soft brown sugar
45 ml (3 tablespoons) blended whisky

Using a saw-bladed knife take a deep cap off the top of each orange and a small one off the bottom to allow it to stand. With a grapefruit knife loosen the flesh and remove. Take out pips and connecting tissues. Put fruit back into the shells. Blend the softened butter with the sugar and make into six balls. Put a ball in each orange and replace the cap. Stand in a heatproof dish. Bake in a slow oven (325 °F, Gas 3, 160 °C) for 30–35 minutes. When serving put a teaspoon of whisky into each orange.

Whiskied Oranges

3 oranges
30 ml (2 tablespoons) demerara sugar
45 ml (3 tablespoons) whisky

Peel and slice the oranges thinly. Remove pips and pith. In a shallow pan put the sugar and whisky and all the juice run from the cutting of the fruit. Melt over a low heat for 2 minutes. Take off and add the orange slices. Turn up the heat for 2–3 minutes. Arrange the fruit on a shallow dish and pour over the pan juices. Chill. Serve with plenty of whipped cream. *Illustrated opposite page 97.*

Lochend Apple Bake

2 large or 4 small cooking apples
1 cup orange juice
30 ml (2 tablespoons) whisky
25 g (1 oz) butter
25 g (1 oz) soft brown sugar
pinch of cinnamon

Peel and core the apples. Pour the orange juice and whisky over them and leave to soak for $\frac{1}{2}$ hour. Melt the butter and sugar in a small pan. Add the juice and whisky and a pinch of cinnamon. Butter a baking dish and put in the apples. Pour the sugar mix over them and bake in a moderate oven for 25–30 minutes. Serve with cream.

Pineapple Easy

½ fresh pineapple
30 ml (2 tablespoons) whisky
15 ml (1 tablespoon) grenadin
1 cooked pavlova base
200 ml (½ pint) double cream
icing sugar
maraschino cherries

Peel, core and chop the fresh pineapple and set to soak in the whisky and grenadin. After 2 hours taste it, and if not sweet enough, sift over some icing sugar. A ripe pineapple will not need this. Whip and sweeten the cream and put half in the pavlova base. Top with the fruit keeping some pieces for decoration. Put the rest of the cream on top and decorate with reserved pineapple and some maraschino cherries drained and dried on a paper towel.

Pavlova Base
4 egg whites
pinch of salt
200 g (8 oz caster sugar)
1 tablespoon cornflour
1 teaspoon vinegar

Beat the whites until stiff with a pinch of salt. Add 6 tablespoons of the sugar and beat again until stiff. Sift the rest of the sugar along with the cornflour onto the mix and add also the vinegar. Fold in carefully with a wire balloon whisk. Mark an 8-inch round on the underside of a sheet of non-stick paper cut to fit a baking sheet. Pile the mixture on this round and spread to the edge of the ring. Form a small volcano shape slightly hollowed in the middle and about 2 inches deep. Bake at 325 °F (Gas 3) for ½ hour and turn the oven off. Leave in the oven for ½ hour. Cool on a wire tray.

Peach Fool

4 fresh peaches
30 ml (2 tablespoons) whisky
10 ml (2 teaspoons) sugar
30 ml (2 tablespoons) water
200 ml ($\frac{1}{2}$ pint) double cream
50 g (2 oz) chopped browned almonds

Put peaches in a bowl and pour boiling water on them to cover. Stand for a minute and peel. Take out the stones and poach the peaches in the whisky, sugar and water. Cool and sieve. Mix with an equal quantity of half-whipped cream. Pile into glasses. Decorate with chopped browned almonds and serve with sponge fingers.

Prunes in Whisky Jelly

$\frac{1}{2}$ kg (1 lb) prunes
100 g (4 oz) sugar
30 ml ($\frac{1}{2}$ oz) gelatine
$\frac{1}{2}$ cup (3 fl oz) whisky

Soak the prunes in water to cover overnight. Add the liquid to the sugar and bring to the boil. Simmer for 3–4 minutes. Add the fruit and stew gently until cooked. Strain off the juice and make up to 300 ml ($\frac{1}{2}$ pint) with water. Soak the gelatine in 50 ml ($\frac{1}{2}$ gill) cold water to dissolve. Add to the juice along with the whisky. Stone and quarter the prunes. Put the fruit and jelly into a ring mould. Allow to set, and then turn out. Fill the middle with whipped cream. *Illustrated opposite page 97.*

Crabbies Green Ginger Jelly

100 ml ($\frac{1}{4}$ pint) water
15 ml ($\frac{1}{2}$ oz) gelatine
rind and juice of 1 lemon
150 ml (5 fl oz) blended whisky
15 ml (3 teaspoons) sugar
200 ml (7 fl oz) green ginger wine
cream to decorate

Dissolve the gelatine in the water and leave with lemon rind to infuse. Strain and dissolve the sugar in it before adding lemon juice, whisky and green ginger wine. Add a drop of green colouring if liked and pour into tall glasses to set. Before serving top each one with a good thick layer of whipped sweetened cream.

Cold Chestnut Soufflé

4 eggs
3 egg yolks
$\frac{1}{2}$ cup sugar
30 ml (2 tablespoons) gelatine
$\frac{1}{4}$ cup blended whisky
1 cup sweetened chestnut purée
200 ml ($\frac{1}{2}$ pint) double cream
marrons glacé

Put the eggs and yolks and sugar in a bowl and beat until very thick. Soften 2 tablespoons gelatine in 4 tablespoons water and add the whisky. Fold into the egg mix when slightly cool, with the chestnut purée and the half-whipped cream. Have an 8-inch soufflé dish ready with a greaseproof paper collar tied round the top and pour in the mix. When set and chilled remove the collar. Decorate with cream noisettes and whole marrons glacé.

Mac's Cold Soufflé

---

5 eggs
75 g (3 oz) caster sugar
30 ml (2 tablespoons) lemon juice
30 ml (2 tablespoons) Crabbie's green ginger wine
15 ml (1 tablespoon) blended whisky
30 ml (2 tablespoons) gelatine
100 ml (1 gill) water
200 ml ($\frac{1}{2}$ pint) double cream

Separate the eggs and beat the yolks until light and fluffy. Add the sugar. Beat in the lemon juice and the wine and whisky. Dissolve the gelatine in the water. Beat the egg whites until stiff and half-whip the cream. Stir the gelatine mix into the yolks. Using a wire whisk fold in the cream first, and then the egg whites. Pour into a prepared soufflé dish and leave to set. Decorate with whipped cream rosettes.

Souffle Café

---

4 eggs
3 yolks
$\frac{1}{4}$ cup sugar
30 ml (2 tablespoons) gelatine

90 ml (6 tablespoons) water
45 ml (3 tablespoons) whisky
45 ml (3 tablespoons) instant coffee
100 ml ($\frac{1}{4}$ pint) whipped cream

Put the eggs, yolks and sugar into a bowl and beat until thick and light. Melt the gelatine in the water and the whisky, and then add the instant coffee. Strain onto the egg mix and fold in using a balloon whisk. Lastly fold in the cream and pour into a soufflé dish to set. Decorate with rosettes of cream and browned chopped almonds. This is very light.

Chocolate Orange and Whisky Mousse

1 chocolate orange (Terry's)
30 ml (2 tablespoons) orange juice
15 ml (1 tablespoon) water
3 eggs
10 ml ($1\frac{1}{2}$ teaspoons) whisky
pinch of salt
crystallized violets

Put the broken-up chocolate orange in a bowl with the orange juice and water and set to melt over a pan of hot water. Separate the eggs. Whisk the whites with a pinch of salt until stiff. When chocolate is just melted but not hot blend in the yolks using a wooden spoon. Beat in the whisky also. Using a balloon whisk fold in the whites very carefully. Pour into little Pots de Crème dishes and set in fridge to chill. Decorate with crystallized violets.

South American Whisky Mousse (Columbia)

3 eggs
15 ml (1 oz) gelatine
$\frac{1}{4}$ cup cold coffee
$\frac{1}{2}$ cup sugar
200 ml ($\frac{1}{2}$ pint) double cream
30 ml (2 tablespoons) whisky
30 ml (2 tablespoons) Kahlua
1 teaspoon vanilla

Separate the eggs. Put the gelatine in the cold coffee to dissolve and then over low heat to melt. Beat the yolks and the sugar until light. Beat the egg whites and the cream until half-whipped. Fold the gelatine, whisky, Kahlua and vanilla into the yolk mix. Fold in the cream and then the whites. Pour into little dishes to set. Decorate with chocolate coffee beans.

Damson Jam and Whisky Omlette

20 ml (1 heaped tablespoon) damson jam
5 ml (1 teaspoon) whisky
2 eggs for each person
10 ml (2 teaspoons) icing sugar
pinch of salt
10 g ($\frac{1}{2}$ oz) butter

Put the jam and whisky in a very small pan and heat. Separate the eggs. Beat yolks with salt until thick. Beat whites and sugar until stiff. Fold the yolks with the whites using a balloon whisk. Melt the butter in an omelette pan. Pour in the egg mix and cook over a gentle heat until soft underneath and then slip under the grill to set the top. Pour on the jam and whisky and fold over gently. Slip onto a plate and dredge with icing sugar and serve at once. Serves 1.

Iced Pudding Cake

150 g (6 oz) glacé fruit
30 ml (2 tablespoons) whisky
30 ml (2 tablespoons) orange juice
Victoria sponge made in oblong loaf tin
200 ml ($\frac{1}{2}$ pint) double cream
5 ml (1 teaspoon) sugar
apricot jam
50 g (2 oz) browned flaked almonds

Soak the glacé fruits in the whisky overnight. Drain and chop the fruit. Add orange juice to the whisky. Slice the cake in 3 or 4 layers lengthwise. Soak each layer with some of the liquid. Whip the cream and sugar and fold in the chopped fruit. Layer with the cream. Heat the apricot jam and brush all over. Put on the almonds. Set in the freezer for 2 hours. Serve in slices with pouring cream.

Tobermory Tartlets

200 g (8 oz) plain flour
pinch of salt
85 ml (3 fl oz) oil
30 ml (2 tablespoons) water
100 g (4 oz) raisins
100 ml (5 tablespoons) whisky
1 cup sugar
$\frac{1}{4}$ cup butter
3 eggs
150 g (6 oz) chopped walnuts
1 teaspoon vanilla
caster sugar

Sift flour and salt in a bowl and add the oil and water.
Mix to a firm dough and knead lightly on a table dusted
with flour. Cover and chill for 15 minutes. Roll out and
use to line 12 3-inch tartlet tins. Soak the raisins in 4
tablespoons of the whisky. Cream the butter and sugar
and then stir in the beaten egg, fruit, chopped nuts and
vanilla. Fill this mixture into the pastry-lined tins and
bake at 350 °F, Gas 4, 180 °C for 40–45 minutes. Put on
a wire rack to cool and while warm sprinkle with the
rest of the whisky. Dredge with caster sugar.

Tipsy Tarts

200 g ($\frac{1}{2}$ lb) rich short pastry
25 g (1 oz) raisins
10 ml (2 teaspoons) whisky
5 ml (1 teaspoon) water
25 g (1 oz) chopped walnuts

10 g ($\frac{1}{2}$ oz) chopped almonds
60 ml (4 tablespoons) redcurrant jelly
1 egg yolk
caster sugar

Roll out pastry and cut out enough rounds to line some patty tins and lids to fit. Boil the raisins in the whisky and water. Cool. Add the nuts and jelly and fill into the patties. Beat the yolk lightly and brush edges of patties. Put on the lids, press in place and brush the tops with yolk too. Sprinkle with a little caster sugar and bake at 375 °F, Gas 5, 190 °C for 10–15 minutes.

Whisky Drops

75 g (5 oz) bitter cooking chocolate
1 egg yolk
25 g (1 oz) butter
15 ml (1 tablespoon) whisky
chocolate powder (cocoa if preferred)

Melt the chocolate very gently and stir in the egg yolk, butter and whisky. Put on a gentle heat for a moment or two and then cool. Form into very small balls, about half an inch in diameter and roll these either in sweetened chocolate powder or in cocoa. Drop each one into a small paper sweet-case and serve after dinner with the coffee. *Illustrated opposite page 80.*

Index